Cover Photo:
Swedish Meat Balls 19
Norwegian Fruit Soup 29
Sweet-Sour Red Cabbage 42
Swedish Tea Ring 49

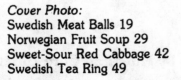
Adventures in Cooking SERIES

Illustrations by Kimanne Core Uhler

Scandinavian Cookbook

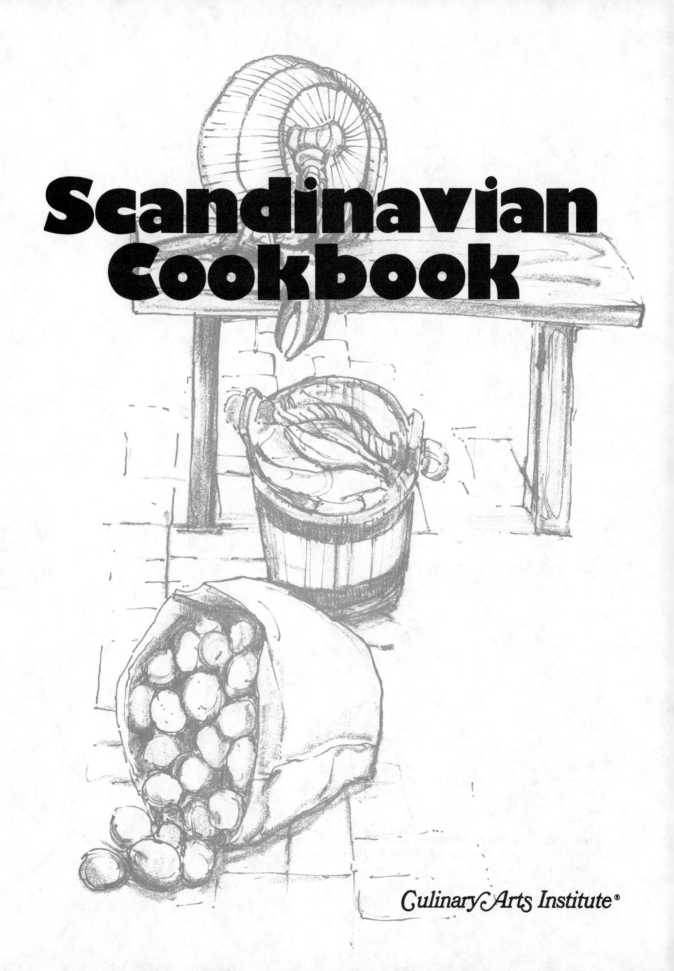

Culinary Arts Institute®

ISBN: 0-8326-0633-2

Contents

Scandanavian Cookery

The Sea-Girt Countries at the top of Europe—Norway, Sweden and Denmark—have developed a cuisine which, though rooted in Continental tradition, has flowered in a way uniquely its own. A robust style of cookery that makes lavish use of energizing foods, Scandinavian cuisine is also colorful, imaginative, and strikingly beautiful in appearance.

To Americans the most familiar aspect of Scandinavian dining traditions is the smorgasbord, far-famed buffet of appetizers, hospitable invitation to hearty sociability. If this has been your introduction to Scandinavian cooking you are already familiar with a fascinating array of hot and cold dishes, meats, cheeses and vegetables, and piquantly seasoned fish, especially herring.

But there is much more to Scandinavian tradition than this first course. There are sauces (richest in the world); dark and delicious breads; cookies, puddings and cakes; open-face sandwiches that are meals in themselves and a joy to behold. Above all, there is the Scandinavian sorcery with fish—bountiful harvest of the cold northern seas which the Scandinavians garner so industriously and cook and garnish so handsomely.

It may seem from the pages that follow that the northern countries' menu is a heroic one, and so it is. With fare like this the hardy ancestors of modern Scandinavia conquered uncharted seas in their open ships and adventured boldly toward a new world.

It's Smart to Be Careful

There's No Substitute For Accuracy

Read recipe carefully.

Assemble all ingredients and utensils.

Select pans of proper kind and size. Measure inside, from rim to rim.

Use standard measuring cups and spoons. Use measuring cups with subdivisions marked on sides for liquids. Use graduated nested measuring cups for dry or solid ingredients.

Check liquid measurements at eye level.

Level dry or solid measurements with straight-edged knife or spatula.

Sift (before measuring) regular all-purpose flour, or not, in accord with the miller's directions on the package. When using the instant type all-purpose flour, follow package directions and recipes. Level flour in cup with straight-edged knife or spatula. Spoon, without sifting, whole-grain types of flour into measuring cup.

Beat whole eggs until thick and piled softly when recipe calls for well-beaten eggs.

Preheat oven at required temperature.

For These Recipes – What To Use

Baking Powder—double-action type.

Bread Crumbs—two slices fresh bread equal about 1 cup soft crumbs or cubes. One slice dry or toasted bread equals about ½ cup dry cubes or ¼ cup fine, dry crumbs.

Buttered Crumbs—soft or dry bread or cracker crumbs tossed in melted butter. Use 1 to 2 tablespoons butter for 1 cup soft crumbs and 2 to 4 tablespoons butter for 1 cup dry crumbs.

Cornstarch—thickening agent having double the thickening power of flour.

Cream—light, table or coffee cream containing 18% to 20% butterfat.

Heavy or Whipping Cream—containing not less than 30% butterfat.

Dressed Fish—head, tail, fins and entrails removed.

Flour—regular all-purpose flour. When substituting for cake flour, use 1 cup minus 2 tablespoons all-purpose flour for 1 cup cake flour.

Grated Peel—whole citrus fruit peel finely grated through colored part only.

Herbs and Spices—ground unless recipe specifies otherwise.

Oil—salad or cooking. Use olive oil only when recipe states.

Rotary Beater—hand-operated (Dover type) beater, or use electric mixer.

Sour Milk—cold sweet milk added to 1 tablespoon vinegar or lemon juice in a measuring cup to fill to 1-cup line; stir. Or use buttermilk.

Sugar—granulated (beet or cane).

Vinegar—cider vingegar.

How To Do It

Baste—spoon liquid (or use baster) over cooking food to add moisture and flavor.

Blanch Nuts—the flavor of nuts is best maintained when nuts are allowed to remain in water the shortest possible time during blanching. Therefore, blanch only about ½ cup at a time; repeat as many times as necessary for larger amounts.

Bring to rapid boiling enough water to well cover shelled nuts. Drop in nuts. Turn off heat and allow nuts to remain in the water about 1 min.; drain or remove with fork or slotted spoon. Place between folds of absorbent paper; pat dry. Gently squeeze nuts with fingers or peel to remove skins. Place on dry absorbent paper. To dry thoroughly, frequently shift nuts to dry spots on paper.

Grate Nuts—use a rotary type grater with hand-operated crank. Follow manufacturer's directions. Grated nuts should be fine and light; do not use an electric blender for grating or grinding nuts called for in these recipes.

Toast Nuts—put blanched nuts in a shallow pan. Heat nuts (plain or brushed lightly with cooking oil) in oven at 350°F until delicately browned. Move and turn occasionally with spoon. Or add blanched nuts to a heavy skillet in which butter (about 1 tablespoon per cup of nuts) has been melted; or use oil. Brown nuts lightly, moving and turning constantly, over moderate heat.

Salt Nuts—toast nuts; drain on absorbent paper and sprinkle with salt.

Boil—cook in liquid in which bubbles rise continually and break on the surface. Boiling temperature of water at sea level is 212°F.

Clean Celery—trim roots and cut off leaves. Leaves may be used for added flavor in soups and stuffings; inner leaves may be left on stalk when serving as relish. Separate stalks, remove blemishes and wash. Proceed as directed in recipe.

Clean Green Pepper—rinse and slice away from pod and stem; trim off any white membrane; rinse away seeds; cut into strips, dice or prepare as directed in recipe.

Clean and Slice Mushrooms—wipe with a clean damp cloth and cut off tips of stems; slice lengthwise through stems and caps.

Clean Onions (dry)—cut off root end and thin slice from stem end; peel and rinse. Prepare as directed in recipe.

Cut Dried Fruits (uncooked) or Marshmallows—use scissors dipped in water.

Dice—cut into small cubes.

Flake Fish—with a fork separate canned (cooked) fish into flakes (thin, layer-like pieces). Remove bony tissue from crab meat; salmon bones are edible.

Flute Edge Of Pastry—press index finger on edge of pastry, then pinch pastry with thumb and index finger of other hand. Lift fingers and repeat procedure to flute around entire edge.

Fold—use flexible spatula and slip down side of bowl to bottom. Turn bowl quarter turn. Lift spatula through mixture along side of bowl with blade parallel to surface. Turn spatula over to fold lifted mixture across material on surface. Cut down and under; turn bowl and repeat process until material seems blended. With every fourth stroke, bring spatula up through center.

Hard-Cook Eggs—put eggs into large saucepan and cover completely with cold or warm water. Cover. Bring water rapidly just to boiling. Turn off heat. If necessary to prevent further boiling, remove pan from heat source. Let stand covered 20 to 22 min. Plunge eggs promptly into running cold water. Roll egg between hands to loosen shell. Start peeling at large end.

Note: Eggs are a protein food and therefore should never be boiled.

Marinate—allow food to stand in liquid (usually oil and acid) to impart additional flavor.

Measure Brown Sugar—pack firmly into dry measuring cup so that sugar will hold shape of cup when turned out.

Measure Granulated Brown Sugar—see substitution table on package before pouring into measuring cup.

Mince—cut or chop into small, fine pieces.

Panbroil Bacon—place a cold skillet only as many bacon slices as will lie flat. Cook slowly, turning frequently. Pour off fat as it collects. When bacon is evenly crisped and browned, remove from skillet and drain on absorbent paper.

Prepare Quick Coffee—for one cup coffee beverage, put 1 teaspoon concentrated soluble coffee (instant) into cup. Add boiling water and stir until coffee is completely dissolved. For one cup double-strength coffee beverage, increase concentrated soluble coffee to 1 tablespoon.

Prepare Quick Broth—dissolve in 1 cup hot water, 1 chicken bouillon cube for chicken broth or 1 beef bouillon cube or ½ teaspoon concentrated meat extract for meat broth.

Rice—force through ricer, sieve or food mill.

Scald Milk—heat in top of double boiler over simmering water or in a heavy saucepan over direct heat just until a thin film appears.

Sieve—force through coarse sieve or food mill.

Simmer—cook in a liquid just below boiling point; bubbles form slowly and break below surface.

Sweeten Whipped Cream—beat thoroughly chilled whipping cream in chilled bowl with chilled rotary beater; beat until cream stands in soft peaks when beater is slowly lifted upright. With final few strokes, beat in 3 tablespoons sifted confectioners' sugar and 1 teaspoon vanilla extract for each cup of whipping cream.

Unmold Gelatin—run tip of knife around top edge of mold to loosen. Invert mold onto chilled plate. If necessary, wet a clean towel in hot water and wring it almost dry. Wrap hot towel around mold for a few seconds only. (If mold does not loosen, repeat.)

Water Bath, Hot—set a baking pan on oven rack and place the filled baking dish in pan. Surround with very hot water to at least 1-inch depth.

Oven Temperatures

Very slow	250°F to 275°F
Slow	300°F to 325°F
Moderate	350°F to 375°F
Hot	400°F to 425°F
Very Hot	450°F to 475°F
Extremely Hot	500°F to 525°F

Use a portable oven thermometer to double-check oven temperature.

When You Broil

Set temperature control of range at Broil. Distance from top of food to source of heat determines the intensity of heat upon food.

When You Deep Fry

About 20 min. before ready to deep fry, fill a deep saucepan one-half to two-thirds full with hydrogenated vegetable shortening, all-purpose shortening, lard or cooking oil for deep frying. Heat fat slowly to temperature given in the recipe. A deep-frying thermometer is an accurate guide for deep-frying temperatures.

If thermometer is not available, the following bread cube method may be used as a guide. A 1-in. cube of bread browns in 60 seconds at 350°F to 375°F.

When using an automatic deep fryer, follow manufacturer's directions for fat and timing.

A Check-List for Successful Baking

Read Again "It's Smart To Be Careful—There's No Substitute for Accuracy"

Place Oven Rack so top of product will be almost center of oven. Stagger pans so no pan is directly over another and they do not touch each other or walls of oven. Place single pan so that center of product is as near center of oven as possible.

Prepare Pan—For cakes with shortening and cake rolls, grease bottom of pan only; line with waxed paper cut to fit bottom of pan only; grease waxed paper. For cakes without shortening (sponge type), do not grease or line pan. For most quick breads, usually grease bottom of pan only or lightly grease baking sheet. If recipe states "set out pan," do not grease or line pan.

Have All Ingredients at room temperature unless recipe specifies otherwise.

Sift (before measuring) regular all-purpose flour, or not, in accord with the miller's directions on the package. When using the instant type all-purpose flour, follow package directions and recipes. Level flour in cup with straight-edged knife or spatula. Spoon, without sifting, whole-grain types of flour into measuring cup.

Cream Butter (alone or with flavorings) by stirring, rubbing or beating with spoon or electric mixer until softened. Add sugar in small amounts creaming thoroughly after each addition. Thorough creaming helps to insure a fine-grained cake.

Beat Whole Eggs until thick and piled softly when recipe calls for well-beaten eggs.

Beat Egg Whites as follows: **Frothy**—entire mass forms bubbles; **Rounded peaks**—peaks turn over slightly when beater is slowly lifted upright; **Stiff peaks**—peaks remain standing when beater is slowly lifted upright.

Beat Egg Yolks until thick and lemon-colored if recipe calls for well-beaten egg yolks.

When Liquid and Dry Ingredients are added to batters, add alternately, beginning and ending with dry. Add dry ingredients in fourths, liquid in thirds. After each addition, beat only until smooth. Finally beat only until batter is smooth (do not overbeat). Scrape spoon or beater and bottom and sides of bowl during mixing.

If using an electric mixer, beat mixture at a low speed when alternately adding liquid and dry ingredients.

Fill Cake Pans one-half to two-thirds full.

Tap Bottom of Cake Pan sharply with hand or on table to release air bubbles before placing in oven.

Apply Baking Tests when minimum baking time is up. For tortes or cakes, touch lightly at center; if it springs back, they are done. Or, insert a cake tester or wooden pick in center; if it comes out clean, they are done.

Cool Tortes 15 min. in pan on cooling rack after removing from oven; cool sponge-type and other cakes as recipe states.

Remove Tortes from pan after cooling. Run spatula gently around sides of pan. Cover with cooling rack. Invert and remove pan. Turn right side up immediately after peeling off waxed paper. Cool cake completely before frosting.

Fill Tortes—Spread filling or frosting over top of bottom layer. Cover with the second layer. Repeat procedure if more layers are used. If necessary, hold layers in position with wooden picks; remove when filling is set.

Frost Filled Tortes—Frost sides first, working rapidly. See that frosting touches plate all around bottom, leaving no gaps. Pile remaining frosting on top of cake and spread lightly.

Test for lukewarm liquid (80°F to 85°F) by placing a drop on wrist; it will feel neither hot nor cold.

Knead Dough by folding opposite side over toward you. Using heels of hands, gently push dough away. Give it one-quarter turn. Repeat process rhythmically until the dough is smooth and elastic, 5 to 8 min., using as little additional flour as possible. Always turn the dough in the same direction.

Remove Rolls, Bread and Cookies from pans as they come from the oven, unless otherwise directed. Set on cooling racks to cool.

Keep Tops of yeast loaves and rolls soft by immediately brushing with butter as they come from the oven.

How To Cook Vegetables

Wash fresh vegetables, but do not soak them in water for any length of time. If they are wilted, put them in cold water for a few minutes.

Baking—Bake such vegetables as potatoes, tomatoes and squash without removing skins. Pare vegetables for oven dishes, following directions given with recipes.

Boiling—Have water boiling rapidly before adding vegetables. Add salt at beginning of cooking period (¼ teaspoon per cup of water). After adding vegetables, again bring water to boiling as quickly as possible. If more water is needed, add boiling water. Boil at a moderate rate and cook vegetables until tender.

In general, cook vegetables in a covered pan, in the smallest amount of water possible and in the shortest time possible. Exceptions for amounts of water or for covering are:

Asparagus—arranged in tied bundles with stalks standing in bottom of a double boiler containing water to cover lower half of spears—cover with inverted double boiler top.

Broccoli—trimmed of leaves and bottoms of stalks. If stalks are over 1 in. in diameter, make lengthwise gashes through them almost to flowerets. Cook quickly in a covered skillet or saucepan in 1 in. of boiling, salted water 10 to 15 min., or just until tender.

Cabbage (mature)—cooked, loosely covered, in just enough water to cover. Cabbage (young)—cooked, tightly covered, in a minimum amount of water (do not overcook).

To restore color to red cabbage, add a small of vinegar at end of cooking period, just before draining.

Cauliflower(whole head)—cooked, uncovered, in a 1 in. depth of boiling, salted water for 5 min.,then covered, 15 to 20 min.

Mature Root Vegetables (potatoes, rutabagas, parsnips)—cooked, covered, in just enough boiling salted water to cover vegetables.

Spinach—cooked, covered, with only the water which clings to leaves after final washing.

A desirable boiled vegetable is free from excess water, retains its original color and is well seasoned. Pieces are uniform and attractive.

Broiling—Follow directions with recipes.

Frying and Deep Frying—Follow directions with specific recipes.

Panning—Finely shred or slice vegetables. Cook slowly until just tender in a small amount of fat, in a covered, heavy pan. Occasionally move with spoon to prevent sticking and burning.

Steaming—Cooking in a pressure saucepan is a form of steaming. Follow directions given with saucepan because overcooking may occur in a matter seconds.

*Note:*Some saucepans having tight-fitting covers may lend themselves to steaming vegetables in as little as 1 teaspoon water, no water or a small amount of butter or shortening.

Canned Vegetables—Heat to boiling in liquid from the can.

Home–canned Vegetables—Boil 10 min.(not required for tomatoes or sauerkraut).

Dried (dehydrated) Vegetables—Soak and cook as directed in specific recipes.

Frozen Vegetables—Do not thaw before cooking (thaw corn on cob and partially thaw spinach). Break frozen block apart with fork during cooking. Cook in as little boiling salted water as possible. Follow directions on package.

Smörgåsbord

Best-known of all Scandinavian dining customs is the smörgåsbord—usually the prelude to the feast, but on some occasions the whole feast itself. In Sweden, where the custom is believed to have originated in the festivities of country people, the smörgåsbord is served as a first course. A small number of appetizers,which invariably include herring, are presented buffet-style to guests who relax and nibble, exchange toasts and conversation, and then assemble around the dining table with appetites pleasantly stimulated but unimpaired. In other countries, and especially in America, the character and the function of the smörgåsbord have altered and it may comprise the principal part of a meal. A munificent variety of fish, meat, cheese, egg and vegetables dishes is arranged on a necessarily commodious buffet or table and guests visit it as often as they please. A dessert (by recommendation simple) and good strong coffee bring the feast to a close.

A time-tried ritual is prescribed for the proper enjoyment of either a small smorgasbord or the full-scale, panoramic affair. First, and always first if one is to observe the Scandinavian spirit of the occasion, the herring! Then one adventures (with clean plate in hand) through dishes in which fish is combined with other ingredients, then cold meats, the delicious hot dishes, the salads and aspics, and finally, for digestion's sake and to soothe a possibly jaded palate, a bit of cheese.

In Norway, the smörgåsbord is also called koldt bord. It usually consists of a few appetizers—fish, meat and cheese—but on special occasions may be elaborate and bountiful, including roasts of meat and several kinds of fish. Roast beef tenderloin, for example, and loin of pork served with prunes and apple slices; boiled lobster with mayonnaise, whole baked or boiled salmon with sour cream; and a whole cold ham. Include parsley potatoes in the more elaborate type of smorgasbord. Rum pudding usually rounds out these heroic collations.

A Swedish adaptation of the smorgasbord is the gracious supé—a late supper served after the theater or an evening of dancing. The supé too is governed to some extent by tradition. Hot dishes are always served. They may be croustades with creamed filling, an omelet or soufflé, new potatoes with fresh dill. Breads, especially the fragrant limpa, accompany the dishes. Fish and a relish, such as sliced tomatoes, are included as a matter of course. Amounts served are not lavish. The dishes are kept small, but always garnished with the flair for beauty that characterizes Scandinavian cuisine. Cookies are sometimes included in supé and coffee is always served. To precede a Swedish dinner, a plate of three (it must be three) canapés is placed before each individual. Canapes would not be served with a smorgasbord.

The smörgåsbord recipes here have been selected with a deep bow to Scandinavian tradition and an understanding nod to some American food preferences. The fruit molds, cream-cheese aspics, macaroni and cole slaw salad would probably not be found on a smörgåsbord table in Stockholm, except perhaps at the height of the tourist season.

The American homemaker can make a respectable gesture toward a smörgåsbord with herring, sardines, anchovies or other small canned fish, a platter of ready-to-serve meats and cheese and a relish or two—all of which may also be included in a much more elaborate buffet.

A word about bread and cheeses: Custom dictates that only the dark breads belong to the smorgasbord and that knäckebröd (hardtack in American parlance) should be among them. Cheese may be Swiss, Danish Bleu, Edam, goat cheeses or bond ost, but it is never proffered in slices. Guests cut it to individual preference.

Pickled Herring

3 qts. cold water
2 salt herring, cleaned and cut into fillets.
1 large onion
1 cup cider vinegar
1 cup water
1 tablespoon peppercorns
1 bay leaf

1. Pour 3 qts. cold water into a large bowl.
2. Put herring into the water. (See Herring Salad on page 15, *To Prepare Herring.*) Set aside to soak 3 hrs.
3. Clean onion and thinly slice.
4. Separate onion slices into rings.
5. Mix cider vinegar, water, peppercorns, and bay leaf together.
6. Drain herring and cut into 2-in. square pieces. Put a layer of herring into a shallow bowl and top with some of the onion rings. Repeat layers of herring and onion. Pour over the vinegar-water mixture. Chill thoroughly in refrigerator several hours or overnight to blend flavors.
7. When ready to serve, drain off liquid. Toss herring and onion lightly to mix and put into a serving bowl. Garnish with sprigs of parsley.

10 to 12 servings

Herring Salad

2 qts. cold water
1 salt herring, cleaned and cut into fillets
½ lb. boneless veal for stew, cut in ½-in. cubes
3 cups water
1 lb. (about 5) medium-size beets
2 small (about ½ lb.) potatoes
3 eggs
2 medium-size onions
1 large apple, rinsed and diced
1½ tablespoons white vinegar
½ teaspoon sugar
½ teaspoon salt
Few grains pepper
1 cup chilled whipping cream

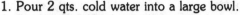

1. Pour 2 qts. cold water into a large bowl.
2. Put herring into the water.
3. Set aside to soak 3 hrs.
4. *To Prepare Herring*—With a sharp knife cut off and discard head. Slit along underside of the fish from head to tail. Remove entrails and scrape insides well. Cut off tail and fins. Rinse thoroughly in cold water. Cut off a strip about ½ in. wide along each of cut edges. Discard strips. Make a slit along backbone just to the bone. Using a sharp knife, carefully pull and scrape the blue skin from the flesh. Be careful not to tear fish. Then cut along backbone through bone and flesh to remove one side of fish. Repeat for the second side. Remove as many of the small bones as possible without tearing fish.
5. *For Salad*—Set out veal for stew.
6. Put 3 cups water into a saucepan.
7. Cook over medium heat about 1 hr., or until meat is tender. Drain; chill in refrigerator.
8. Meanwhile, leaving on 1- 2-in. stem and the root end, cut off leaves from beets.
9. Scrub beets thoroughly. Cook 30 to 45 min., or until just tender. When beets are tender, drain. Plunge beets into running cold water; peel off and discard skin, stem and root end. Cut beets into slices ¼ in. thick. Cut slices into strips ¼ in. wide. Set in refrigerator to chill.
10. While beets cook, wash and scrub potatoes with a vegetable brush.
11. Cook about 20 min., or until the potatoes are tender when pierced with a fork. Drain potatoes. To dry potatoes, shake pan over low heat. Peel potatoes and dice. Chill in refrigerator.
12. Hard-cook eggs.
13. Cut 2 of the peeled eggs into halves lengthwise. Finely chop the egg whites and egg yolks separately and set aside. Cut the remaining peeled egg into slices crosswise. Set aside.
14. Put a bowl and beater in refrigerator to chill.
15. Clean onions and finely chop.
16. Drain the herring, dry on absorbent paper, and cut into ½-to ¾-in. pieces. Put the herring, veal, potatoes, and onion into a large bowl with apple.
17. Pour over ingredients in bowl and mixture of white vinegar, sugar, salt and pepper.
18. Toss lightly to coat evenly.
19. Using the chilled bowl and beater, beat whipping cream until cream is of medium consistency (piles softly).
20. Turn the whipped cream over the herring mixture and toss lightly until thoroughly combined. Add the beets and mix thoroughly, being careful not to break the strips. Turn into a serving bowl and chill thoroughly in refrigerator. If desired, turn Herring Salad into a 2-qt. mold. Pack lightly. Chill thoroughly.
21. When ready to serve, spoon the chopped egg white around the edge of the salad, the chopped egg yolk over the center. Arrange the hard-cooked egg slices in a circle between the chopped egg white and egg yolks. Complete the garnish with sprigs of **parsley.** Place a cruet of **white vinegar,** colored with beet juice, and a cruet of **cream** on the table so that each person may sour the salad to his own taste.

10 to 12 servings

Fish Balls

2	tablespoons butter
¼	cup sifted all-purpose flour
1	teaspoon salt
⅛	teaspoon pepper
1	cup cream
3	cups flaked cooked fish (cod, trout, fillet of sole, whitefish)
1	egg yolk, beaten
2	eggs, slightly beaten
1	cup fine, dry bread crumbs

1. Set out a deep saucepan or automatic deep-fryer and heat fat to 350°F.
2. Heat butter over low heat in a saucepan.
3. Blend in flour, salt and pepper.
4. Heat until mixture bubbles. Add cream gradually, stirring constantly.
5. Cook rapidly, stirring constantly, until mixture thickens. Remove from heat; cool.
6. Meanwhile, flake finely enough cooked fish to yield 3 cups.
7. When sauce is cool, blend in the fish and 1 egg yolk.
8. Shape mixture into balls 1 in. in diameter. Dip balls into 2 eggs.
9. To coat evenly, roll balls in bread crumbs.
10. Deep-fry Fish Balls in heated fat. Deep-fry only as many balls at one time as will float uncrowded one-layer deep in the fat. Turn balls often. Deep-fry 2 min., or until lightly browned. Drain; remove to absorbent paper.
11. Keep Fish Balls warm for the smorgasbord.

About 5 doz. Fish Balls

"Boiled" Salmon

5-	lb. piece salmon, dressed
3	qts. water
¼	cup lemon juice
3	tablespoons salt
	Sauce for Salmon (on this page)
	Sprigs of parsley
	Lemon wedges

1. Set out a large sauce pot having a tight-fitting cover and a rack.
2. Have salmon ready.
3. Place salmon on a length of cheesecloth and tie ends securely.
4. Bring water, lemon juice, and salt to boiling in the sauce pot.
5. Lower the fish carefully into the sauce pot so that it rests on the rack. Cover and simmer 10 to 15 min., or until fish flakes. Carefully lift fish from sauce pot. Place on a large platter or baking sheet to cool. Chill in the refrigerator.
6. Meanwhile, prepare Sauce for Salmon.
7. When ready to serve, remove fish carefully from cheesecloth and place on a serving platter. Scrape off skin (if any). Garnish with parsley and lemon wedges.
8. Serve with the sauce.

10 to 12 servings.

Sauce for Salmon

½	cup thick sour cream
1	teaspoon prepared horse-radish
¼	teaspoon salt
¼	teaspoon sugar

1. Blend sour cream, horse-radish, salt and sugar together thoroughly.
2. Chill thoroughly in refrigerator.

About ½ cup sauce

Rolled Fish Fillets

Sauce for Lobster (page 18)
1½ **lbs. fish fillets (sole, cod, halibut, haddock)**
3 **cups water**
1½ **teaspoons salt**
Pimiento
Sprigs of parsley

1. Prepare sauce for lobster and chill in refrigerator.
2. Set out fish fillets. (If using frozen fish fillets, thaw according to directions on package.) Cut fillets with a sharp knife into strips 10x1-in. Starting with the narrow end, roll fillets tightly and fasten with a wooden pick. Put fish rolls into a sauce-pan with water and salt.
3. Bring to boiling. Reduce heat and simmer 6 to 8 min., or until fish flakes. Carefully remove fish rolls from liquid with a slotted spoon. Drain on absorbent paper. Chill in refrigerator.
4. When ready to serve, remove wooden picks and arrange fish rolls on a serving platter. Cover with the sauce. Garnish with pimiento and parsley.

About 2 doz. fish rolls

Fish in Aspic

Tomato Aspic (page 26)
1½ **cups cooked fish pieces (herring, fillet of sole, or trout)**
Sprigs of parsley

1. Lightly oil a 1½-qt. mold with salad or cooking oil (not olive oil). Set aside to drain.
2. Prepare Tomato Aspic.
3. Chill in refrigerator or in a pan of ice and water until mixture is consistency of thick, unbeaten egg white. (If mixture is placed over ice and water, stir frequently; if placed in refrigerator, stir occasionally.)
4. Meanwhile cut into 1-in. pieces enough cooked fish to yield 1½ cups.
5. When mixture is of desired consistency, blend in the fish and turn into the mold. Chill in refrigerator until firm.
6. When ready to serve, unmold onto a chilled serving platter and garnish with parsley.

8 to 10 servings

"Boiled" Lobster

Hot salted water (1 tablespoon salt per qt. water)
1   live lobster, about 1½ lbs.
Fresh dill or parsley
Sauce for Lobster (on this
page)

1. Fill a large deep kettle or sauce pot having a tight-fitting cover about ⅔ full (or enough to cover the lobster) with hot salted water.
2. Bring water rapidly to boiling. Grasp lobster by the back and plunge head first into the water.
3. Cover, bring water again to a rolling boil. Reduce heat and simmer 15 to 20 min. Drain and cover with cold water to chill. Drain again. Place shell-side down on a cutting board.
4. Twist off the two large claws, the smaller ones and the tail. With a pair of scissors cut or with a sharp knife slit the bony membrane on the underside of tail. Remove and discard the intestinal vein. Using a sharp knife, cut completely through tail crosswise into 1½ in. pieces. With a sharp knife, cut lobster into halves; cut completely through entire lengh of body and through shell. Remove and discard the intestinal vein running lengthwise through center of body. Remove and discard stomach (a small sac which lies in the head) and spongy lungs (which lie in upper body cavity between meat and shell).
5. If present, remove and reserve the tomalley (green liver) and the coral (bright red roe) to be used along with lobster meat or as a garnish. Using a sharp knife, cut the body crosswise into 1½ in. pieces.
6. Chill pieces of lobster and the claws in refrigerator. When ready to serve on the smorgasbord, arrange pieces of lobster and claws on a platter, shell-side up, to resemble a whole lobster. Garnish lobster with fresh dill or parsley.
7. Serve with Sauce for Lobster.

About 8 to 10 servings

Note: To use cooked lobster meat in food preparation, do not cut lobster into pieces. Spread tail shell apart and remove meat in one piece; remove meat from body shell. Disjoint the large claws and crack with a nutcracker. A nut pick may be helpful in removing meat from small joints and claws. Chill in refrigerator, cut and use as desired.

1¼ cups lobster meat

Sauce for Lobster

1   cup mayonnaise
¼   cup lemon juice
1   tablespoon sugar

1. Blend together throughly the mayonnaise, lemon juice, and sugar.
2. Chill in refrigerator.

1¼ cups sauce

Cooked Shrimp

1	lb. fresh shrimp with shells
2	cups water
2	tablespoons lemon juice
2	teaspoons salt
1	bay leaf
	Fresh dill or parsley

1. Wash shrimp in cold water.
2. Drop shrimp into a boiling mixture of water, lemon juice, salt, and bay leaf.
3. Cover tightly. Simmer 5 min., or only until shrimp are pink and tender. Drain and cover with cold water to chill. Drain shrimp again.
4. To peel shrimp, remove the tiny legs. Peel shells from shrimp. Cut a slit to just below surface along back (outer curved surface) of shrimp to expose the black vein. With knife point, remove vein in one piece. Rinse shrimp quickly in cold water. Drain on absorbent paper. Store in refrigerator until ready to use.
5 To serve shrimp on the smorgasbord, pile the shrimp into a bowl and hang some of the shrimp on the rim of the bowl. Garnish with fresh dill or parsley.

1½ to 2 doz. Cooked Shrimp

Swedish Meat Balls I

1	cup (3 slices) fine, dry bread crumbs
1	lb. ground round steak
½	lb. ground pork
½	cup mashed potatoes
1	egg, beaten
1	teaspoon salt
½	teaspoon brown sugar
¼	teaspoon pepper
¼	teaspoon allspice
¼	teaspoon nutmeg
⅛	teaspoon cloves
⅛	teaspoon ginger
3	tablespoons butter

1. Set out a large, heavy skillet having a tight-fitting cover.
2. Set out bread crumbs.
3. Lightly mix together in a large bowl ½ cup of the bread crumbs and steak, pork, potatoes, egg and a mixture of salt, brown sugar, pepper, allspice, nutmeg, cloves, and ginger.
4. Shape mixture into balls about 1 in. in diameter. Roll balls lightly in remaining crumbs.
5. Heat the butter in the skillet over low heat.
6. Add the meat balls and brown on all sides. Shake pan frequently to brown evenly and to keep balls round. Cover and cook about 15 min., or until meat balls are thoroughly cooked.
7. Keep meat balls hot for the smorgasbord.

About 3 doz. meat balls

Swedish Meat Balls II: To serve meat balls for dinner, follow recipe for Swedish Meat Balls I. Prepare 1 cup **Quick Meat Broth.** Remove meat balls from skillet after browning. Blend 2 tablespoons **flour,** ¼ teaspoon **salt,** and few grains **pepper** into the contents of the skillet. Heat until mixture bubbles. Stirring constantly, gradually add 1 cup **cream** and the meat broth. Return the meat balls to the skillet and cover. Simmer 30 min. Serve the meat balls in the gravy.

6 servings

Jellied Veal

2	lbs. veal shank
1	lb. veal shoulder
2	qts. boiling water
1	tablespoon salt
10	peppercorns
1	bay leaf
¾	teaspoon ginger
¼	teaspoon pepper
	Lingonberry preserves or Pickled Beets (page 23)

1. Set out a 9½x5¼x2¾ in. loaf pan.
2. Set out veal shank and shoulder.
3. Put meat into a large, heavy sauce pot with water, salt, peppercorns and bay leaf.
4. Bring to boiling. Skim off any foam. Cover, reduce heat and simmer slowly about 2 hrs., or until meat is tender. Remove meat from broth and set aside.
5. Strain the broth and return it to the sauce pot. Bring to boiling and boil rapidly, uncovered, until 1 qt. liquid remains.
6. Meanwhile, remove the meat from the bone. Put through the medium blade of a food chopper. Add the meat to the broth with ginger and pepper.
7. Turn into the loaf pan and set aside to cool.
8. Chill in refrigerator until firm.
9. When ready to serve, unmold onto a chilled serving plate. Slice and serve with Lingonberry preserves or Pickled Beets.

10 to 12 servings

Roast Ham

10-	lb. smoked whole ham
1	cup firmly packed brown sugar
1	tablespoon all-purpose flour
1	teaspoon dry mustard
2	tablespoons cider vinegar
	Whole cloves

1. Set out a shallow roasting pan with a rack.
2. Follow roasting directions on wrapper or as given below for ham.
3. Place ham fat side up on rack. Insert roast meat thermometer in center of thickest part of lean, being sure bulb does not rest on bone or in fat.
4. Roast uncovered at 300°F 2½ hrs.
5. Meanwhile, prepare glaze.
6. For Glaze—Mix together in a small bowl brown sugar, flour and dry mustard.
7. Stir cider vinegar in to form a smooth paste.
8. To Glaze Ham— Remove ham from oven after it has roasted 2½ hrs. Remove rind (if any), being careful not to remove fat. Making diagonal cuts, score fat surface of ham to make a diamond pattern. Place whole cloves in centers of diamonds.
9. Spread glaze over ham. Return to oven and continue roasting about 45 min., or until internal temperature of ham reaches 160°F. (Total roasting time is about 3 hrs., allowing 18 to 20 min. per pound.)
10. Remove ham from oven. Allow ham to cool completely. Remove thermometer. Cut ham into slices and press slices together again to resemble a whole ham.

20 servings

Smoked Beef Tongue

4-   lb. smoked beef tongue
Whole apple celery leaves

1. Put tongue into a large kettle or a sauce pot having a tight-fitting cover.
2. Add enough boiling water to cover the tongue. Cover and simmer 3 to 4 hours, or until tender. (If necessary, add more boiling water to keep the tongue covered during cooking period.) Or follow cooking directions on the wrapper.
3. When tongue is tender, slit skin on underside of tongue and peel it off. Cut away roots and gristle. (Plunging tongue into cold water after cooking helps to loosen the skin.) Return tongue to cooking liquid to complete cooling. Drain and chill in refrigerator.
4. Cut chilled tongue into thin slices and arrange on a serving platter. Garnish with whole apple and celery leaves.

9 to 10 servings

Rolled Rib Roast of Beef

7-   lb. rolled rib roast of beef
1½   teaspoons salt
⅛   teaspoon pepper

1. Set out a shallow roasting pan with a rack.
2. Have beef ready.
3. Place roast on rack in roasting pan, fat-side up. Sprinkle with a mixture of salt, and pepper.
4. Insert roast meat thermometer in center of thickest part of lean; be sure bulb does not rest in fat.
5. Roast at 300°F allowing about 32 min. per pound for rare; about 38 min. per pound for medium; and about 48 min. per pound for well done. Roast will be done when roast meat thermometer registers 140°F for rare; 160°F for medium; and 170° for well done.
6. For use on smorgasbord, cool roast completely. Remove roast meat thermometer. Cut a few slices and arrange with the roast on a platter.

12 to 14 servings

Roast Loin of Pork with Prunes

3- lb. loin of pork
1 teaspoon salt
¼ teaspoon pepper
2 cups water
1½ cups (about 9 oz.) prunes
   Apple slices

1. Set out a roasting pan with a rack.
2. Have pork ready.
3. Rub meat with a mixture of salt
4. Place loin of pork on rack in roasting pan. Insert roast meat thermometer at top center of pork loin, being sure that bulb rests in center of the loin and not on bone or in fat.
5. Roast pork uncovered at 325°F until internal temperature reaches 170°F. The total roasting time should be 1½ to 1¾ hrs. Allow 30 to 35 min. per pound.
6. Meanwhile, bring water to boiling in a large saucepan.
7. Add prunes.
8. Cover and simmer about 15 min., or until prunes are partially tender. Drain prunes and cut into halves. Remove and discard pits.
9. About ½ hr. before roast is done, arrange prunes around pork loin. Continue roasting for ½ hr.
10. Remove pork loin from oven; cool completely. Remove thermometer from meat.
11. When ready to serve for smorgasbord, slice the meat and arrange on a serving platter. Garnish with the prunes and **apple slices.**

8 to 10 servings

Liver Paste

1½ lbs. liver (beef, veal or pork)
1 cup hot water
2 eggs, slightly beaten
1 cup cream
¼ cup sifted all-purpose flour
2 teaspoons salt
¼ teaspoon white pepper
⅛ teaspoon ginger
   Few grains nutmeg
3 slices bacon
4 anchovy fillets, drained of oil
1 slice onion
   Pickled Beets (page 23)

1. Grease an 8½x4½x2½-in. loaf pan.
2. Cut away tubes and outer membrane, if necessary, from liver (beef, veal or pork).
3. Put liver in skillet with water.
4. Cover and simmer 5 min. Drain and cool.
5. Meanwhile, combine and mix eggs, cream, flour, salt, white pepper, cloves, ginger and nutmeg lightly.
6. Force the cooled liver through the medium blade of a food chopper with bacon, anchovy fillets and onion.
7. Mix lightly with the egg mixture, blending thoroughly. Pack into the greased loaf pan.
8. Bake at 350°F 1½ to 2 hrs.
9. Cool completely on cooling rack.
10. When ready to serve, loosen meat gently from sides of pan with spatula. Invert onto platter. Cut into thin slices and garnish with Pickled Beets.

10 to 12 servings

Stuffed Eggs

6	eggs
¾	teaspoon dry mustard
½	teaspoon salt
¼	teaspoon pepper
1	tablespoon finely chopped onion
1	tablespoon lemon juice
2	tablespoons thick sour cream or mayonnaise
	Pimiento

1. Hard-cook eggs.
2. Cut peeled eggs into halves lengthwise. Remove egg yolks to a bowl. Set egg whites aside.
3. Force egg yolks through sieve or ricer, or mash with fork. Stir in mixture of dry mustard, salt and pepper.
4. Blend in onion and lemon juice.
5. Stir in sour cream or mayonnaise, moistening egg-yolk mixture to a smooth, thick consistency.
6. Spoon mixture lightly into egg whites, leaving tops rounded. Or force mixture through a pastry bag and a No. 7 decorating tube into egg whites. Garnish center of egg with pimiento.
7. Chill eggs in the refrigerator.

12 servings

For Variety—Blend in one of the following: ¼ teaspoon **savory** or **tarragon**; 1 tablespoon **prepared horse-radish**; 1 table-spoon chopped **parsley** or **chives.**

Pickled Beets

1	lb. (about 5) medium-size beets
1	medium-size onion
¾	cup cider vinegar
¾	cup reserved beet liquid
1	whole clove

1. Leaving on 1-to-2-in. stem and the roof end, cut off leaves from beets.
2. Scrub beets thoroughly. Cook in water to cover 30 to 45 min., or until just tender. When beets are tender, drain, reserving liquid in a measuring cup for liquids.
3. Plunge beets into running cold water; peel off and discard skin, stem and root end. Cut beets into slices ¼ in. thick.
4. Clean and thinly slice onion.
5. Separate the onion slices into rings.
6. Put a layer of beets into a shallow bowl. Cover with some of the onion rings. Repeat layers of beets and onions, ending with the beets. Pour over a mixture of vinegar, beet liquid, and whole clove.
7. Cover and chill thoroughly in refrigerator several hours or overnight to blend flavors.

8 to 10 servings

Hot Potato Salad

12	medium-size (about 4 lbs.) potatoes, cut in halves
2	tablespoons butter
4	egg yolks, beaten
¼	cup cream
4	teaspoons cider vinegar
1	tablespoon salt
2	teaspoons sugar
1	teaspoon pepper
¼	cup chopped parsley
¼	cup chopped onion
	Sprigs of parsley
	Pickled Beets cut in strips
	Lemon slices

1. Wash, pare and cook potatoes.
2. Cook about 20 min., or until tender when pierced with a fork. Drain.
3. To dry potatoes, shake pan over low heat. To heat potato masher, food mill or ricer and a mixing bowl, scald them with boiling water. Mash or rice potatoes thoroughly. If necessary, keep potatoes hot over simmering water.
4. Meanwhile, cream butter until softened.
5. Blend in egg yolks, cream, cider vinegar and a mixture of salt, sugar and pepper.
6. Stir in chopped parley and onion.
7. Add the hot mashed potatoes and mix until thoroughly blended. Turn into a warm serving dish. Garnish with Sprigs of parsley, beets and lemon slices.

8 to 10 servings

Cucumber Salad

1	large cucumber
⅓	cup cider vinegar
5	tablespoons water
5	tablespoons sugar
½	teaspoon salt
	Few grains white pepper
1	tablespoon finely chopped parsley

1. Rinse and pare cucumber.
2. Score cucumber by pulling the tines of a fork lengthwise through cucumber. Cut cucumber into very thin slices. Put into a shallow bowl.
3. Mix well cider vinegar, water, sugar, salt and pepper.
4. Pour over the cucumber slices and toss lightly to coat evenly. Cover and put in the refrigerator for several hours to chill and allow flavors to blend.
5. Garnish cucumbers with parsley.

8 to 10 servings

Cabbage Salad

⅓	cup mayonnaise
⅓	cup French dressing
1	teaspoon dry mustard
¼	teaspoon curry powder
¼	teaspoon salt
¾	lb. cabbage (about 3 cups, shredded)
	Pimiento
	Sprigs of parsley

1. Blend together thoroughly in a small bowl mayonnaise, French dressing, dry mustard, curry powder and salt.
2. Cover and put in refrigerator to chill.
3. Wash and finely shred or chop cabbage.
4. Put cabbage into a deep bowl, cover and put in refrigerator to chill.
5. Shortly before serving time, remove cabbage and dressing from refrigerator. Stir dressing and pour enough of it over cabbage to moisten. Toss lightly to blend. Add more dressing if necessary.
6. Put cabbage into a serving bowl and shape into a mound. Garnish with pimiento and parsley.

About 6 servings

Fruit-Filled Gelatin Salad

1	cup mayonnaise
1½	tablespoons lemon juice
¼	cup chilled whipping cream
2½	tablespoons sifted confectioners' sugar
1	20-oz. can crushed pineapple (about 1½ cups, drained)
1	16 oz. can sliced peaches (about 1¼ cups drained)
2	medium-size oranges Orange juice (enough to make 2 cups liquid)
2	3-oz. pkgs. cherry-flavored gelatin
2	cups very hot water
¼	cup lemon juice

1. For Lemon Mayonnaise—Set a bowl and beater in refrigerator to chill.
2. Set out mayonnaise.
3. Blend in 1½ tablespoons lemon juice.
4. Using the chilled bowl and beater, beat whipping cream until it is of medium consistency (piles softly).
5. With final few strokes, beat or blend in confectioners sugar.
6. Fold into mayonnaise mixture.
7. For Salad—Drain reserving syrup in a 2-cup measuring cup for liquids, contents of can crushed pineapple and can sliced peaches.
8. Rinse oranges. With a sharp knife, cut away peel and white membrane. Remove sections by cutting on either side of dividing membranes; remove, section by section, over the measuring cup to collect juice.
9. Put fruit into a bowl, cover, and put in refrigerator until ready to use.
10. Add orange juice to reserved syrup.
11. Empty gelatin into a large bowl.
12. Add water stirring constantly.
13. Stir until gelatin is completely dissolved; blend in the reserved fruit and lemon juice.
14. Chill in refrigerator or in pan of ice and water until gelatin mixture is slightly thicker than consistency of thick, unbeaten egg white. (If mixture is placed over ice and water, stir frequently; if it is placed in the refrigerator, stir occasionally.)
15. Lightly oil a 1½-qt. fancy mold with salad or cooking oil (not olive oil). Set it aside to drain.
16. When gelatin is of desired consistency, stir in the pineapple, peaches, and orange sections. Turn mixture into prepared mold. Place in refrigerator to chill until firm.
17. Unmold onto chilled serving platter. Serve with the Lemon Mayonnaise.

About 12 servings

Jewel Mold: Follow recipe for Fruit-Filled Gelatin Salad. Omit fruit. Substitute 2 cups **orange juice** for the 2 cups fruit syrup. Pour mixture into a prepared 1-qt. fancy mold and chill until firm.

About 8 servings

Tomato Aspic — Cream Cheese Salad Ring

Tomato Aspic Ring
Cream Cheese Ring
Salad dressing

4	cups tomato juice
1/3	cup chopped celery leaves
1/3	cup chopped onion
2 1/2	tablespoons sugar
1 1/2	teaspoons salt
1/2	bay leaf
1/2	cup cold water
2	env. unflavored gelatin
2 1/2	tablespoons cider vinegar
1/2	cup cold water
1	env. unflavored gelatin
9	oz. cream cheese
2	cups thick sour cream
4	teaspoons lemon juice
1 1/2	tablespoons sugar
1	teaspoon salt

1. Two identical 1-qt. ring molds with be needed.
2. For Salad Ring—Prepare and chill until firm Tomato Aspic Ring and Cream Cheese Ring.
3. When ready for serving, unmold the Tomato Aspic Ring onto a chilled plate large enough for the aspic to be expanded to twice its size. Cut aspic into 1-in. slices and spread slices about 1-in. apart.
4. Unmold Cream Cheese Ring onto a second chilled plate. Cut into 1-in. slices. Transfer slices to the alternating spaces between the tomato aspic slices. Arrange so that a perfect ring is formed again.
5. Place on plate in the center of salad ring a small bowl of salad dressing.
6. For Tomato Aspic Ring—Pour tomato juice into a saucepan.
7. Add to tomato juice celery leaves, onion, 2 1/2 tablespoons sugar, 1 1/2 teaspoon salt and bay leaf.
8. Simmer uncovered, 10 min.
9. Meanwhile, pour 1/2 cup cold water into a small bowl.
10. Sprinkle unflavored gelatin evenly over cold water.
11. Set aside.
12. Lightly oil one ring mold with salad or cooking oil (not olive oil). Set it aside to drain.
13. Remove tomato juice mixture from heat. Strain liquid into a large bowl. Immediately add the softened gelatin to tomato juice mixture and stir until gelatin is completely dissolved. Add cider vinegar and stir well.
14. Pour mixture into the prepared mold. Cool and place in refrigerator to chill until frim.
15. For Cream Cheese Ring—Lightly oil the second mold with salad or cooking oil (not olive oil). Set it aside to drain.
16. Pour 1/2 cup cold water into a small saucepan.
17. Sprinkle 1 env. unflavored gelatin evenly over cold water.
18. Set the saucepan over low heat and stir constantly until gelatin is completely dissolved. Remove from heat.
19. Beat cream cheese until very soft.
20. Mix in sour cream, lemon juice, 1 1/2 tablespoons sugar, and 1 teaspoon salt in order (adding cream gradually and stirring until smooth after each addition.)
21. Blend dissolved gelatin into cream cheese mixture. Turn mixture into the prepared mold. Place in refrigerator to chill until firm.

About 24 servings

Tomato Aspic Squares: Follow recipe for Tomato Aspic-Cream Cheese Salad Ring. Omit salad ring and Cream Cheese Ring. Set out a l3x9x2-in. pan. Pour **Tomato Aspic** into pan, cool and chill in refrigerator until firm. When ready to serve, cut into 2-in. squares. Beat 1 1/2 oz. (1/2 pkg.) **cream cheese,** softened, and 1 tablespoon **milk** until fuffy. Force cream cheese through a pastry bag and No. 27 decorating tube onto center of each square. Arrange squares on a serving tray and garnish with sprigs of parsley.

About 2 doz. aspic squares

Fish Fondue

12	frozen fish sticks
1	lb. mussels (shelled and cooked)
½	lb. shrimp (cleaned and cooked)
½	lb. lobster meat (cleaned and cooked)
1	quart vegetable (or peanut) oil

Dill Mustard Sauce

¼	cup beef broth
3	tbsp. dry mustard
2	tbsp. mayonnaise
1	tsp. dill

Tartar Sauce

¼	cup mayonnaise
½	tsp. dry mustard
2	tbsp. pickle relish

Chili Sauce

¼	cup ketchup
2	tbsp. chili sauce

Batter

1	cup all-purpose flour
¼	tsp. salt

Dip

6	eggs, beaten
½	cup milk

1. Heat oil in fondue pot to 375°F.
2. Spear bite-sized fish and dip fish first into egg-milk mixture, then roll in flour batter.
3. Dip fish carefully into hot oil and cook until golden brown, about 30 seconds to 1 minute.
4. Remove from fondue fork, dip in sauce and enjoy.

6 servings

Soups

Throughout Scandinavia soup is regarded with high seriousness and soup making is a living art. The tureen makes a daily appearance on Scandinavian dining tables and may appear oftener. For Scandinavians are so fond of some of their soups, notably the colorful fruit soups, that they serve them as dessert.

Swedish Fruit Soup I

1   cup (about 6 oz.) dried apricots
¾   cup (about 3 oz.) dried apples
½   cup (about 3 oz.) dried peaches
½   cup (about 3½ oz.) prunes
½   cup (about 2½ oz.) dark seedless raisins
2   quarts water
¼   cup sugar
3   tablespoons quick-cooking tapioca
1   3-in. piece stick cinnamon
1   teaspoon grated orange peel
1   cup red raspberry fruit syrup
    Whipped cream
    Slivered blanched almonds

1. Set out a large sauce pot having a tight-fitting cover.
2. Set out apricots, apples, peaches, prunes and raisins.
3. With a sharp paring knife, remove pits from prunes. Put fruits into the sauce pot with water.
4. Cover and soak fruits 2 to 3 hrs., if desired.
5. Add to the sauce pot sugar, tapioca, cinnamon, and orange peel.
6. Bring to boiling; reduce heat, cover and simmer about 20 min., or until fruit is tender. Remove from heat and stir in raspberry fruit syrup.
7. Chill soup in refrigerator.
8. Serve soup with whipped cream and almonds.

About 3 qts. soup

Swedish Fruit Soup II: Follow recipe for Swedish Fruit Soup I. Omit raisins.

Norwegian Fruit Soup

1   **qt. water**
2   **tablespoons rice**
½   **cup finely chopped apple**
1   **cup pitted dark sweet cherries and juice**
½   **cup red raspberry fruit syrup**
¼   **cup lemon juice**
2-in.   **piece stick cinnamon**
1   **tablespoon cold water**
1   **teaspoon cornstarch**

1. Bring 1 qt. water to boiling in a deep saucepan.
2. Add 2 tablespoons rice to water so boiling will not stop. (The Rice Industry no longer considers it necessary to wash rice before cooking.) Boil rapidly, uncovered, 15 to 20 min., or until a kernel is entirely soft when pressed between fingers. Drain rice, reserving liquid.
3. Rinse and finely chop enough apple to yield ½ cup.
4. Put cherries into a bowl.
5. Add fruit syrup and lemon juice.
6. Return the rice water to the saucepan. Add the apple and cinnamon stick.
7. Cook over medium heat 4 to 5 min., or until apple is tender. Add the drained rice and the cherry mixture. Remove the cinnamon. Simmer 5 min.
8. Blend together cold water and cornstarch to form a smoth paste.
9. Blend cornstarch mixture into soup. Bring to boiling. Continue to cook 3 to 5 min. Cool soup slightly.
10. Serve soup warm or cold. If serving soup cold, garnish with **whipped cream.**

About 3½ cups soup

Raisin Fruit Soup: Follow recipe for Norwegian Fruit Soup. Omit cherries. Increase red raspberry syrup to 1 cup. Add to the syrup mixture 1 cup (about 5 oz.) dark seedless **raisins.**

Yellow Pea Soup with Pork

¾   **lb. (about 1⅔ cups) yellow peas**
2½   **qts. cold water**
1   **l-lb. piece smoked shoulder roll**
3   **qts. water**
¾   **cup coarsely chopped onion**
1   **teaspoon salt**
1   **teaspoon whole thyme**
¼   **teaspoon sugar**

1. Rinse, sort (discarding imperfect peas) and put peas into a large saucepan.
2. Pour 2½ qts. cold water over the peas.
3. Cover and set peas aside to soak overnight.
4. The next day, set out shoulder roll.
5. Put the shoulder roll, water and onion into a large sauce pot.
6. Simmer 1½ to 2 hrs., or until meat is tender.
7. Remove meat and set aside. Skim off fat from liquid, leaving about 2 tablespoons. Drain the peas and add to the broth with salt, whole thyme, and sugar.
8. Simmer 1½ to 2 hrs., or until peas are tender. If necessary, skim off shells of peas as they come to the surface.
9. Serve soup with thin slices of the meat.

About 2½ qts. soup

Norwegian Vegetable Soup

2	lbs. beef short ribs
1	lb. soup bone
3	qts. cold water
1	tablespoon salt
1½	cups (3 medium-size) coarsely chopped onion
1¼	cups (3 medium-size) coarsely chopped carrots
1	small head (1 lb.) cabbage, cut in pieces
1	whole nutmeg
2	beef bouillon cubes
2½	teaspoons salt
¼	teaspoon pepper
½	cup finely chopped parsley
2	cups Medium White Sauce (double recipe, page 44; substitute the broth for the milk; stir into sauce 4 teaspoons sugar, 2 tablespoons vinegar, and 2 tablespoons prepared horseradish)

1. Set out ribs and soup bone.
2. Put water and 1 tablespoon salt into a large sauce pot.
3. Bring to boiling; reduce heat and simmer 2½ hrs. During cooking, occasionally remove foam that forms on top.
4. Prepare onion, carrots, and cabbage.
5. After simmering soup 1 hr. add the chopped onion. Continue to simmer 1 hr. longer. Add the carrots and cabbage. Simmer another ½ hr.
6. Skim off fat from soup, leaving about 2 tablespoons. Add nutmeg.
7. Simmer 15 min. longer. Remove the short ribs and soup bone to a bowl. Remove and discard the nutmeg. Stir in bouillon cubes until dissolved, 2½ teaspoon salt, and pepper.
8. Remove 2 cups of the broth. Stir parsley into the remaining soup.
9. Keep soup hot while preparing sauce for meat.
10. Prepare Medium White Sauce.
11. Add the meat and cook over low heat until heated thoroughly.
12. Serve the soup first. Then serve the meat and sauce.

8 to 10 servings

Vegetable Soup with Tomatoes: Follow recipe for Norwegian Vegetable Soup. Rinse 4 medium-size **tomatoes.** Cut out stem ends and cut tomatoes into six pieces. Add tomatoes with bouillon cubes.

Buttermilk Soup

3	eggs
½	cup sugar
2	tablespoons grated lemon peel
2	qts. buttermilk

1. Beat eggs until very thick and piled softly.
2. Add sugar gradually, beating thoroughly after each addition.
3. Add lemon peel.
4. Pour buttermilk over the egg mixture gradually, stirring until blended.
5. Chill in refrigerator about 2 hrs.
6. Serve soup the day it is prepared, preferably soon after chilling.

About 2½ qts. soup

Fish Soup

2	lbs. dressed fish with head (such as cod, trout, or mackerel)
1	qt. water
1	tablespoon salt
2	carrots
1	small onion
2	medium-size potatoes (about ½ lb.)
2	eggs
1	cup thick sour cream
2½	teaspoons salt
	Minced chives

1. Set out a large, heavy saucepan or sauce pot having a tight-fitting cover.
2. Rinse fish in cold water and drain well.
3. Using a sharp, heavy knife cut fish crosswise into 1-in. slices. Break through the bone by tapping the knife with a hammer.
4. Put fish slices and head into the saucepan with water and salt.
5. Bring to boiling. Reduce heat, cover and cook 8 to 10 min., or until fish flakes.
6. Meanwhile, wash, pare or scrape, and dice carrots.
7. Clean and chop onion.
8. Wash, pare and cut potatoes into ½-in. cubes.
9. Cook vegetables in saucepan about 8 min., or until tender. Drain and set aside.
10. When fish is cooked, remove and discard the head. Ladle or spoon out 3 cups of the liquid and set aside. Keep the fish hot.
11. Beat 2 eggs until thick and piled softly.
12. Stir in sour cream and salt.
13. Add the reserved fish liquid very gradually, stirring constantly. Add the vegetables. Cook over low heat until heated. Garnish soup with minced chives.
14. Serve soup first. Drain the fish and serve with **parsley potatoes** (boiled potatoes tossed in a mixture of melted butter and chopped parsley).

6 servings

Dumplings for Soup

1	cup water
¼	cup butter
¼	teaspoon salt
1	cup sifted all-purpose flour
2	eggs
2	qts. water
2	teaspoons salt

1. Bring 1 cup water, butter and ¼ teaspoon salt to a rolling boil.
2. Add flour all at one time.
3. Beat vigorously with a wooden spoon until mixture leaves sides of pan and forms a smooth ball. Remove from heat. Quickly beat in 2 eggs one at a time, beating until smooth after each addition.
4. Continue beating until smooth and thick.
5. Heat 2 qts. water and 2 teaspoons salt to boiling in a large saucepan.
6. Drop dumpling dough by rounded teaspoonfuls into water. (Dough will drip more readily from a spoon moistened in the boiling water.) Cook only as many dumplings at one time as will float, uncrowded, one layer deep. Cook 3 to 5 min., or until dumplings rise to surface of water. Remove dumplings with a slotted spoon. Put several dumplings in each soup plate and spoon or ladle soup over them.

About 3 doz. dumplings

Main Dishes, Vegetables and Salads

Fish of northern European waters—fresh, salted or canned—forms a main part of the Scandinavian menu. Scandinavians have a fondness bordering on reverence for fish, and a skilled hand and lively wit in preparing them. Pork, prized for its flavor, is also popular. Dried fruits are frequently used in meat cookery. Certain dishes are traditional to holidays—goose for Christmas and St. Martin's Day, lutfisk for the Christmas season. The first greens of spring are served in ceremonial spirit, as befits the return of verdure in lands where winters are long.

Norwegian Meat Balls

¼ cup (about ¾ slice) fine, dry bread crumbs
1 cup milk
1 lb. round steak, ground twice
1 egg, beaten
3 tablespoons grated onion
1 teaspoon salt
¼ teaspoon nutmeg
⅛ teaspoon pepper
3 tablespoons butter
½ cup Quick Meat Broth (page 9)
1 large onion
4 tablespoons butter
1 tablespoon sugar

1. Put bread crumbs into a large bowl.
2. Pour milk over the crumbs.
3. Stir until blended. Add to the bowl steak, egg, onion and a mixture of salt, nutmeg and pepper.
4. Mix lightly until thoroughly blended. Shape into patties 2½ in. in diameter and ¼ in. thick.
5. Heat 3 tablespoons butter in a large skillet having a tight-fitting cover.
6. Add the patties to the skillet and cook over medium heat until patties are well browned.
7. Turn to brown second side. Set patties aside in the skillet to keep warm.
8. Prepare Quick Meat Broth and set aside.
9. Clean onion and cut into thin slices.
10. Heat 2 tablespoons butter in a small skillet.
11. Add the onion and cook over medium heat until lightly browned. Remove onion from the skillet and set aside. Drain off any fat. Add sugar to the skillet.
12. Stirring constantly with the back of a wooden spoon, heat until sugar is melted. Add the meat broth gradually and 2 tablespoons of butter.
13. Stir until well blended. Pour over the meat balls. Cover meat with the onion slices. Cover skillet and simmer 10 min.

4 to 5 servings

Note: Norwegian Meat Balls may be served on the smorgasbord.

Norwegian Meat Balls and Gravy

4	tablespoons butter
6	tablespoons finely chopped onion
1	lb. ground beef
¼	lb. ground lean pork
½	cup (½ slice) soft bread crumbs
½	cup milk
1	egg, beaten
2	teaspoons sugar
1¼	teaspoons salt
½	teaspoon nutmeg
¼	teaspoon allspice
3	tablespoons all-purpose flour
1	teaspoon sugar
½	teaspoon salt
¼	teaspoon pepper
1	cup water
1	cup cream

1. For Meat Balls—Heat butter in a large heavy skillet over low heat.
2. Add and cook onion over medium heat until onion is golden yellow, stirring occasionally.
3. Combine and mix together lightly the onion and ground beef, lean pork, bread crumbs, milk, egg and a mixture of sugar, salt, nutmeg and allspice.
4. Shape meat mixture into 1-in. balls.
5. Heat 2 tablespoons butter.
6. Add the meat balls and brown over medium heat. Shake pan frequently to obtain an even browning and to keep balls round. When thoroughly cooked, remove meat balls to warm serving dish; keep warm while preparing gravy.
7. For Gravy—Add to the fat in the skillet a mixture of flour, 1 teaspoon sugar, ½ teaspoon salt, and pepper.
8. Heat until mixture bubbles and flour is lightly browned.
9. Remove from heat; add gradually, stirring in, a mixture of water and cream.
10. Cook rapidly, stirring constantly, until mixture thickens; do not boil. Cook 1 to 2 min. longer. Pour gravy over meat balls in dish.
11. Serve at once.

6 servings

Danish Pork Chops

2	lbs. pork chops
	salt
	pepper
1	tsp. curry
1	lb. lean bacon
2	tart apples
2	yellow onions
1	cup plain yogurt
	paprika powder
1	tsp. butter

1. Cut bacon, onions and apples in strips.
2. Saute in butter over low heat.
3. Brown the chops in butter.
4. Pour on the yogurt, cover and fry the chops slowly for 5 minutes.
5. Distribute the fried bacon, onions and apples on the chops and serve with boiled rice and a green salad.

6 Servings

Danish Meat Balls

1	lb. beef, ground twice
½	lb. pork, ground twice
1	tablespoon finely chopped onion
½	cup sifted all-purpose flour
1	teaspoon salt
¼	teaspoon pepper
1	cup milk
¼	cup water
1	egg, beaten
3	tablespoons butter
	Sweet-Sour Red Cabbage (page 42)

1. Combine in a large bowl beef, pork, onion and a mixture of flour, salt, and pepper.
2. Add gradually, mixing vigorously milk, water and egg.
3. Beat vigorously until mixture is smooth and well blended.
4. Heat butter in a heavy skillet.
5. Using a tablespoon (not measuring spoon), drop the meat mixture by rounded tablespoonfuls into the skillet. (Meat will drop more readily from a spoon dipped in melted butter.) Cook over medium heat until browned. Using a slotted spoon turn meat balls to brown evenly. Allow about 8 to 10 min. to cook meat balls.
6. Serve with **browned potatoes** and Sweet-Sour Red Cabbage.

About 3 doz. small balls

Pork Tenderloin Stuffed with Prunes

1½ lbs. pork tenderloin, in one piece
12 about (3 oz.) prunes
3 tablespoons butter
1 teaspoon salt
Water
Drippings
3 tablespoons fat
3 tablespoons all-purpose flour
¼ teaspoon salt
⅛ teaspoon pepper
1½ cups milk
½ cup drippings

1. Set out a large heavy skillet having a tight-fitting cover.
2. For Meat—Set out pork.
3. Trim off any excess fat. Using a sharp knife cut meat lengthwise about two-thirds through.
4. Set out prunes.
5. Using a sharp knife, remove pits from prunes. Arrange the prunes in the pork tenderloin and fasten with skewers.
6. Heat butter in the skillet.
7. Add the pork tenderloin and cook slowly, turning to brown all sides evenly. When meat is browned, sprinkle over it 1 teaspoon salt.
8. Cover and cook slowly about 1½ hrs., or until meat is tender when pierced with a fork. During cooking add a small amount of water.
9. When meat is tender, remove to a heated platter and carefully remove skewers.
10. For Gravy—Leaving brown residue in pan, pour drippings into a bowl.
11. Allow fat to rise to surface; skim off fat and reserve. Remaining drippings are meat juices which should be used as part of the liquid in making gravy.
12. Measure fat into roasting pan.
13. Blend in flour, salt and pepper until smooth.
14. Stirring constantly, heat until mixture bubbles. Remove from heat and slowly blend in milk and drippings. stirring constantly and vigorously.
15. Return to heat and cook rapidly, stirring constantly, until sauce thickens. Cook 1 to 2 min. While stirring, scrape bottom and sides of pan to blend in brown residue.
16. Serve gravy with the meat.

4 servings

Pork Tenderloin Stuffed with Parsley:

Follow recipe for Pork Tenderloin Stuffed with Prunes. Omit prunes. Rinse and remove stems from about 1 cup **parsley.** Stuff meat with the parsley.

Beef Lindstrom

3	medium-size potatoes (about 1 lb.)
½	cup finely diced Pickled Beets (page 23)
1½	lbs. beef, ground twice
2	egg yolks, beaten
¼	cup cream
2	tablespoons chopped onion
1	tablespoon capers
1	teaspoon salt
¼	teaspoon pepper
3	tablespoons butter

1. Wash and scrub potatoes with a vegetable brush.
2. Cook 30 to 35 min., or until potatoes are tender when pierced with a fork.
3. Meanwhile, finely dice enough pickled beets to yield ½ cup.
4. Mix beef, egg yolks, cream, onion and capers and a mixture of salt and pepper together in a bowl.
5. Drain the potatoes. To dry potatoes, shake over low heat. Peel potatoes and set aside to cool. When potatoes are cooled, finely dice and blend into the meat mixture with the beets. Chill in refrigerator 1 to 2 hrs. to allow flavors to blend thoroughly.
6. Shape the meat mixture into patties about ¾ in. thick.
7. Heat butter in a heavy skillet.
8. Put the meat patties in the skillet and cook over medium heat until brown on one side. Turn and brown other side. Allow 10 to 15 min. for cooking patties.
9. Serve immediately.

6 to 8 servings

Stuffed Cabbage Rolls

1	large head (3 to 3½ lbs.) cabbage
	Boiling water to cover
1	teaspoon salt
1	lb. veal, ground four times
1	lb. beef, ground four times
1¼	cups milk
⅔	cup fine, dry bread crumbs
4	teaspoons grated onion
2½	teaspoons salt
1	teaspoon nutmeg
	Water to cover
	Salt (1 teaspoon per quart of water)
3	tablespoons butter
3	tablespoons all-purpose flour
¾	teaspoon salt
½	teaspoon cardamom
2	cups milk

1. Set out a large sauce pot or kettle having a tight-fitting cover.
2. For Cabbage—Remove and discard wilted outer leaves, rinse and cut core from cabbage.
3. Put cabbage in the sauce pot or kettle and add boiling water to cover and 1 teaspoon salt.
4. Cover and simmer about 5 min., or until leaves are softened. Carefully separate cabbage leaves and set aside on absorbent paper to drain.
5. For Filling—Mix together lightly in a bowl veal, beef, 1¼ cups milk, bread crumbs, onion, 2½ teaspoons salt and nutmeg.
6. For Cabbage Rolls—Place a small cabbage leaf in the center of a large leaf. Drop about ½ cup of the meat mixture onto the center of each small leaf. (Meat mixture will drop more readily from a moist spoon or cup.) Roll each leaf, tucking ends in toward center. Fasten securely with wooden picks or tie with clean string.
7. Bring water to cover and salt (1 teaspoon per quart of water) to boiling in the sauce pot or kettle.
8. Add the cabbage rolls one at a time so that water continues to boil. Reduce heat, cover and cook 20 min., or until tender. Carefully remove rolls with a slotted spoon. Remove wooden picks or string. Place rolls in a serving dish and serve with Cream Gravy.
9. For Cream Gravy—Heat butter in a saucepan over low heat.
10. Blend in flour, ¾ teaspoon salt, and cardamom.
11. Heat until mixture bubbles. Remove from heat. Add 2 cups milk while stirring constantly.
12. Return to heat and bring rapidly to boiling, stirring constantly. Cook 1 to 2 min. longer.

15 cabbage rolls

Lamb in Cabbage

1½	lbs. boneless lamb shoulder, cut in 1-in. cubes
3	cups water
1	head (about 2 lbs.) cabbage
3	tablespoons all-purpose flour
1½	teaspoons salt
1½	teaspoons peppercorns

1. Set out lamb.
2. Put into a large saucepan having a tight-fitting cover. Add water.
3. Cook over medium heat 20 to 30 min., or until just tender.
4. Meanwhile, remove and discard wilted outer leaves from cabbage, rinse and cut into 1-in. pieces (discarding core).
5. When meat is just tender, drain, reserving liquid. Put one-half cabbage into saucepan.
6. Set out a mixture of flour, salt and peppercorns.
7. Sprinkle one-half of mixture over cabbage. Put the meat into the saucepan in an even layer over the cabbage. Add the remaining cabbage and sprinkle remaining half of flour mixture over all. Pour over cabbage 2⅓ cups of the reserved liquid. Cover and cook over low heat about 1½ hrs., or until meat and cabbage are very tender.
8. Serve immediately.

6 servings

Meat Casserole

2	lbs. brisket of beef
¾	lb. fresh ham or lean shoulder of pork
4	large yellow onions
2	oz. salad oil
1	lb. green peppers
1	lb. tomatoes
2	teaspoons salt
2	teaspoons paprika
2	teaspoons freshly ground black pepper
3-4	cloves garlic, pressed
1	bunch parsley

1. Cut the meat in cubes 1″ x 1″ in size.
2. Chop the onions and fry in the oil.
3. Brown the meat cubes in the rest of the oil.
4. Cut the peppers in strips and the tomatoes in wedges and mix with the meat. Add the salt and the other seasonings.
5. Pour on cold water just to cover. Bring to boil and let boil until meat is tender, about 1 to 1½ hours. Serve the casserole sprinkled with chopped parsley.

8 servings

Pork Casserole

14	oz pork fillet
5	oz. chicken liver
1	garlic clove
3	onions
3	tablespoons butter or margarine
	dash freshly ground pepper
1	bayleaf (crushed)
	dash thyme
4	orange slices
4	carrots
½	cup bouillon and ¾ cup red wine
	or 1¼ cup bouillon
	chopped parsley

1. Thaw chicken livers (if you use frozen) and chop. Cut pork in ¼″ thick slices.
2. Chop peeled onion and crush garlic. Peel carrots and cut in pieces.
3. Brown meat, onion and liver separately in butter and then add carrots, seasonings and orange slices with peel left on.
4. Pour bouillon and red wine on mixture and cook over low heat for 20 minutes. Add liver for last 10 minutes of cooking time. Stir carefully.
5. Serve garnished with **chopped parsley.**

4 servings

Finnan Haddie

2	lbs. finnan haddie (smoked haddock)
3	qts. water
2	teaspoons salt
2	eggs
¼	cup butter
	Sprigs of parsley
	Lemon wedges

1. Have finnan haddie ready.
2. Put fish on a length of cheesecloth and tie ends securely. Lower fish into a large sauce pot or kettle and add water and salt.
3. Bring to boiling. Reduce heat and simmer 10 to 15 min., or until fish flakes.
4. Meanwhile, hard-cook 2 eggs.
5. Chop one of the peeled eggs finely and set aside. Cut the other peeled egg into slices crosswise and set aside.
6. When fish flakes, carefully lift from the sauce pot or kettle. Remove the cheesecloth and lift fish onto a warm serving platter.
7. Melt butter over low heat.
8. Remove from heat; add the finely chopped egg and pour over the fish. Garnish with the egg slices and sprigs of parsley and lemon wedges.

6 servings

Perch with Parsley and Dill

8	medium-size perch, dressed
1	teaspoon salt
½	teaspoon pepper
¼	cup finely chopped parsley
2	tablespoons finely chopped parsley
2	tablespoons chopped fresh dill or 1 teaspoon dill seed
¼	cup hot water
	Sprigs of parsley
	Sprigs of dill
	Lemon wedges

1. Butter a 1½-qt. baking dish.
2. Have ready 8 medium-size perch, dressed.
3. Season fish with a mixture of salt and pepper.
4. Cover bottom of baking dish evenly with ¼ cup finely chopped parsley.
5. Arrange the fish in the baking dish. Top with 2 tablespoons finely chopped parsley, and 2 tablespoons chopped fresh dill or 1 teaspoon dill seed.
6. Pour water around the fish.
7. Bake at 350°F. 20 to 25 min., or until fish flakes.
8. Carefully transfer fish to a warm serving platter and garnish with sprigs of parsley, sprigs of dill and lemon wedges.

4 servings

Fish Pudding

2	lbs. fish fillets (haddock, cod)
2	teaspoons salt
½	teaspoon pepper
⅛	teaspoon nutmeg
1½	tablespoons cornstarch
2	tablespoons water
1	cup cream
	Mushroom Sauce (page 44)

1. Butter a 1-qt. casserole. Heat water for hot water bath.
2. Set out fish fillets.
3. Force fish through the medium blade of a food chopper.
4. Mix in salt, pepper, and nutmeg.
5. Blend cornstarch and water togerther to form a smooth paste.
6. Add cream gradually.
7. Blend with fish mixture. Turn into casserole.
8. Bake in the hot water bath at 350°F. 40 to 50 min., or until a silver knife comes out clean when inserted halfway between center and edge of casserole.
9. Serve with Mushroom Sauce.

6 servings

Creamed Shrimp and Lobster over Cauliflower

1	6-oz. can (about 1 cup) lobster meat
1	4½-oz. can (about 1 cup) shrimp
1	medium-size head cauliflower
1	cup Medium White Sauce (page 44)
3	tablespoons reserved lobster liquid
1	tablespoon reserved shrimp liquid

1. Drain reserving liquids separately, contents of cans of lobster and shrimp.
2. Remove any bony tissue from the lobster and cut lobster into pieces. Cut the shrimp into halves lengthwise. Set aside.
3. Prepare, soak and cook cauliflower.
4. Meanwhile, prepare Medium White Sauce.
5. Stir into the sauce the shrimp, lobster, lobster liquid and shrimp liquid.
6. Cook over medium heat until mixture is thoroughly heated.
7. Drain cauliflower and put into a serving bowl. Pour the sauce over the cauliflower and serve immediately.

4 to 5 servings

Baked Kippers

4	medium-size (about 1¼ lbs.) potatoes
2	medium-size onions
4	3¼-oz. cans Norway kippers
3	tablespoons melted butter
4	eggs
2	cups milk
1	teaspoon salt
¼	teaspoon pepper

1. Butter a 2-qt. casserole. Heat water for hot water bath.
2. Wash, pare and cut potatoes into ¼-in. slices.
3. Cook about 10 min., or until potatoes are partially tender. Drain and set aside.
4. Clean onions and cut into ¼-in. slices.
5. Drain on absorbent paper, contents of cans Norway kippers.
6. Cover bottom of casserole with a layer of the partially cooked potatoes. brush with butter.
7. Cover with a layer of the onion slices. Top onions with a layer of kippers. Repeat layers of potatoes, onions and kippers.
8. Beat eggs slightly.
9. Add milk, salt and pepper gradually, stirring constantly.
10. Pour over the fish in the casserole.
11. Bake in the hot water bath at 350°F. 40 min., or until a silver knife comes out clean when inserted halfway between center and edge of casserole.
12. Garnish with sprigs of parsley and serve immediately.

6 to 8 servings

Creamed Kippers and Mushrooms

4   3¼-oz. cans Norway kippers
3   cups Mushroom Sauce (three times recipe, page 44)
    Sprigs of parsley
    Toast triangles

1. Drain Norway kippers on absorbent paper.
2. Cut into 1-in. pieces and set aside.
3. Prepare 3 cups Mushroom Sauce.
4. Add the kippers and heat thoroughly.
5. Turn into a warm serving dish or casserole and garnish with sprigs of parsley.
6. Serve with toast triangles.

6 servings.

Creamed Bacon and Onion

2   large onions (about 2 cups, diced)
½   lb. bacon
2   cups milk
3   tablespoons all-purpose flour
½   teaspoon salt
⅛   teaspoon pepper
    Boiled potatoes

1. Clean onions and dice.
2. Cut bacon into 1-in. pieces.
3. Put the bacon and onion into a skillet. Cook over medium heat, moving and turning frequently with a spoon until onion is golden brown and bacon is evenly crisped and browned. Pour off excess fat as it collects.
4. Meanwhile, put milk into a screw-top jar.
5. Sprinkle flour, salt and pepper evenly over milk.
6. Cover jar tightly; shake until well blended.
7. When bacon and onion are done, remove skillet from heat. Stirring constantly. slowly pour the milk-flour mixture into the skillet. Return to heat and bring to boiling. Reduce heat and simmer 3 to 5 min., keeping mixture moving gently with a spoon.
8. Serve over boiled potatoes.

4 servings.

Creamed Salt Pork and Onion: Follow recipe for Creamed Bacon and Onion. Substitute ½ lb. **salt pork,** diced, for the bacon.

Roast Goose

½	lb. prunes
3	cups water
1	goose, 10 to 12 lbs., ready-to-cook weight
	Salt
6	medium-size (about 2 lbs.) apples

1. Set out a shallow roasting pan with rack.
2. Put into a large saucepan prunes and water.
3. Bring to boiling; reduce heat and simmer about 10 min., or until prunes are partially tender. Drain prunes and remove pits. Set aside to cool.
4. Meanwhile, clean and remove any layers of fat from body cavity and opening of goose.
5. Cut off neck at body leaving on neck skin. (If goose is frozen, thaw according to directions on package.) Rinse and pat dry with absorbent paper. (Reserve giblets for use in other food preparation.)
6. Rub cavities of goose with salt.
7. Wash apples, pare, quarter, and core.
8. Lightly fill body and neck cavities with the apples and prunes. To close body cavity, sew or skewer and lace with cord. Fasten neck skin to back with skewer. Loop cord around legs and tighten slightly. Place breast-side down on rack in roasting pan.
9. Roast uncovered at 325°F. 3 hrs. Remove fat from pan as it accumulates during this period. Turn goose breast-side up. Roast 1 to 2 hrs. longer, or until goose tests done. To test for doneness, move leg gently by grasping end of bone; drumstick-thigh joint should move easily. (Protect fingers with paper napkin.) Allow about 25 min. per pound for total roasting time.
10. To serve, remove skewers and cord. Place goose on heated platter. Remove some of the apples and prunes from the goose and arrange on the platter.

8 servings

Bacon Pancake

1	cup sifted all-purpose flour
1	tablespoon sugar
½	teaspoon salt
2	eggs, slightly beaten
2	cups milk
½	lb. bacon
	Lingonberry preserves

1. Sift flour, sugar and salt together and set aside.
2. Blend eggs and milk together.
3. Gradually add the milk mixture to the dry ingredients, stirring until well blended. Set aside about 1 hr.
4. Grease well an 11x7x1½-in. baking dish.
5. Dice bacon and pan broil.
6. Add the bacon to the batter and stir until blended. Pour into the baking dish.
7. Bake at 400°F. 40 to 45 min., or until mixture is browned.
8. Cut into squares and serve with Lingonberry preserves.

6 servings

Soufflé with Mushroom Sauce

2	cups Thick White Sauce (double recipe, page 44)
4	egg yolks
4	egg whites
½	cup milk
½	lb. mushrooms
1	medium-size onion (about ¼ cup, finely chopped)
2	tablespoons butter

1. For Soufflé—Set out a 1½-qt. casserole; do not grease. (If necessary, a 1-qt. casserole with straight sides may be used; fold a 2-ft. piece of waxed paper in half lengthwise. Place waxed paper around casserole, cut-side down, overlapping ends of waxed paper. Secure waxed paper around casserole by tying with string.)

2. Prepare 2 cups thick White Sauce.

3. Beat egg yolks until thick and lemon-colored.

4. Slowly spoon 1 cup of the sauce into egg yolks, while stirring vigorously. Cool to lukewarm. Set remaining white sauce aside.

5. Beat eggs whites until rounded peaks are formed and egg whites do not slide when the bowl is partially inverted.

6. Gently spread sauce over beaten egg whites. Carefully fold together until just blended. Turn mixture into casserole. Insert the tip of a spoon 1 in. deep in casserole, 1 to 1½ in. from edge; with spoon run a line around mixture to form a circle.

7. Bake at 325°F. about 45 to 50 min., or until a silver knife comes out clean when inserted halfway between edge and center of casserole.

8. For Sauce—Add milk to the reserved white sauce, stirring in until blended.

9. Set aside.

10. Clean and finely chop mushrooms, and onion.

11. Heat butter in a skillet.

12. Add the mushrooms and onion to the skillet. Cook over medium heat until onion is transparent and mushrooms are lightly browned and tender; with a spoon, move and turn frequently. Add to the white sauce, mixing in thoroughly.

13. Cook over low heat until thoroughly heated.

14. Serve soufflé immediately with the mushroom sauce.

6 servings

Soufflé with Asparagus Sauce: Follow recipe for Soufflé with Mushroom Sauce. Substitute **asparagus** for the mushrooms. Clean, cut into pieces, and cook 1½ lbs. asparagus. Drain asparagus. Mix into sauce with cooked onion.

Soufflé with Spinach Sauce: Follow recipe for Soufflé with Mushroom Sauce. Substitute **spinach** for the mushrooms. Clean and cook 2 lbs. spinach. Drain spinach and chop. Mix into sauce with cooked onion.

Swedish Potato Dumplings

6	medium-size (about 2 lbs.) potatoes, cut in halves
1	egg yolk, slightly beaten
1½	teaspoons salt
¾	lb. lean salt pork, bacon, or ham
1	medium-size onion, chopped
3	cups sifted al-purpose flour
2	qts. water
2	teaspoons salt
	Melted butter

1. Wash potatoes, pare and cook.
2. Cook about 20 min., or until potatoes are tender when pierced with a fork. Drain.
3. To dry potatoes, shake pan over low heat. Mash or rice potatoes thoroughly. Whip in egg yolk and 1½ teaspoons salt until potatoes are fluffy.
4. Set potatoes aside.
5. Cut salt pork, bacon, or ham into cubes or 1-in. pieces.
6. Put into a skillet with onion.
7. Cook over medium heat, moving and turning with a spoon. Pour off fat as it collects. When meat is evenly crisped and browned and onion is golden brown, remove from skillet and drain on absorbent paper.
8. Measure flour.
9. Add about one-half the flour to the potato mixture, blending thoroughly. Add enough remaining flour to make a soft dough.
10. Turn out on a floured surface and knead as for bread dough. Using hands, pat out dough ½ in. thick. Cut into 2-in. rounds using a lightly floured 2-in. round biscuit cutter. Spoon about 2 teaspoons of the bacon-onion mixture into the center of one half the rounds. Cover with the other rounds. Seal edges securely and shape into balls.
11. Bring water and 2 teaspoons salt to boiling in a large heavy saucepan.
12. Gradually add dumplings to boiling water so that boiling does not stop. Cook only as many dumplings at one time as will float, uncrowded, one layer deep. Cook 15 min. Remove with a slotted spoon; drain over water a few seconds.
13. Put into a warm serving dish and serve with melted butter.

About 2 doz. dumplings

Fried Potato Dumplings: Follow recipe for Swedish Potato Dumplings, or use leftover dumplings. Heat in a skillet 3 tablespoons **butter.** Add the dumplings and cook over medium heat until browned, moving and turning with a spoon to brown evenly.

Sweet-Sour Red Cabbage

1	head (about 2 lbs.) red cabbage
	Boiling salted water to cover (1 teaspoon salt per quart of water)
½	cup firmly packed brown sugar
1	tablespoon caraway seed
½	cup vinegar
¼	cup butter

1. Set out a heavy 3-qt. saucepan.
2. Remove and discard wilted outer leaves from red cabbage.
3. Rinse, cut into quarters (discarding core), and coarsely shred (about 2 qts., shredded). Put cabbage into the saucepan and add water to cover, brown sugar, caraway seed.
4. Cook 8 to 12 min., or until cabbage is just tender. Remove from heat and drain.
5. Add to cabbage vinegar and butter.
6. Toss together lightly to mix.
7. Serve immediately.

6 servings

Brown Beans

1½   qts. water
2⅓   cups (about 1 lb.) brown beans or kidney beans
1   cup dark corn syrup
¼   cup cider vinegar
1   tablespoon salt
    Swedish Meat Balls (page 19)

1. Heat water to boiling in a large, heavy saucepan having a tight-fitting cover.
2. Meanwhile, wash and sort beans.
3. Add beans gradually to water so boiling will not stop. Reduce heat, cover and simmer 2 min. Remove saucepan from heat and set the beans aside for 1 hr.
4. Return saucepan to heat, cover and simmer about 1¾ hrs. stirring once or twice, until beans are tender. If necessary, add hot water to keep beans covered with liquid.
5. When beans are tender, add to the saucepan corn syrup, vinegar and salt.
6. Blend thoroughly and cook uncovered over medium heat 45 min., or until sauce has thickened.
7. Serve hot with fried salt pork or Swedish Meat Balls.

6 servings

Danish Cabbage

2   lbs. green cabbage
3   cups boiling water
1   cup sour cream
1   tsp. caraway seed
½   tsp. salt
½   tsp. white pepper

1. Cook cabbage in boiling water covered 6-8 minutes until tender, but still crisp. Drain very well.
2. In the top of a double boiler toss cabbage with sour cream, caraway seed, salt and pepper. Cover and cook for 15 minutes.

6 servings

Tomato Cabbage

3   cups cabbage
¾   cup boiling water
4   slices bacon
1   small yellow onion, minced
1   cup tomato puree
½   tsp. salt
½   tsp. white pepper
2   tsp. brown sugar

1. Cut cabbage into shreds.
2. Boil milk and gradually drop in cabbage. Boil for 2 minutes. Drain and discard milk.
3. While the cabbage is boiling dice and saute bacon. Remove bacon from pan and set aside.
4. Saute onion in bacon fat. Add tomato puree, salt, pepper and brown sugar.
5. Bring sauce to a boil and add the cabbage and bacon. Serve very hot.

6 servings

Lettuce and Sour Cream Salad

1 medium-size head lettuce
1 cup thick sour cream
1 tablespoon plus 1 teaspoon sugar
1 tablespoon vinegar
1 tablespoon grated onion
2 teaspoons prepared horseradish
1 teaspoon salt
Finely chopped parsley
Paprika

1. Cut out core and discard bruised leaves, rinse with cold water and drain lettuce well.
2. Chill lettuce in refrigerator.
3. Blend together thoroughly sour cream, sugar, vinegar, onion, horseradish and salt.
4. Chill thoroughly in refrigerator.
5. When ready to serve, tear lettuce into bite-size pieces and put into a bowl. Spoon the sour cream mixture over the lettuce and toss lightly to coat thoroughly. Sprinkle finely chopped parsley around outer edge of salad.
6. Sprinkle center of salad with paprika.
7. Serve immediately.

6 servings

Lettuce and Whipped Cream Salad:

Follow recipe for Lettuce and Sour Cream Salad. Omit sour cream mixture. Put a bowl, beater and 1½ cups **whipping cream** into the refrigerator to chill. When ready to serve salad, beat the cream, using the chilled bowl and beater until it is of medium consistency (piles softly). Beat in with final few strokes 3 tablespoons **sugar** and ¼ teaspoon **salt.** Gently stir in 1 tablespoon **vinegar.** Omit paprika.

Medium White Sauce

2 tablespoons butter
2 tablespoons all-purpose flour
¼ teaspoon salt
Few grains pepper
1 cup milk

1. Heat butter in a saucepan over low heat.
2. Blend in flour, salt and pepper.
3. Heat until mixture bubbles. Remove from heat. Add milk gradually, stirring in.
4. Cook rapidly, stirring constantly, until sauce thickens. Cook 1 to 2 min. longer.

About 1 cup sauce

Thick White Sauce: Follow recipe for Medium White Sauce, using 3 to 4 tablespoons **flour** and 3 to 4 tablespoons **butter.**

Mushroom Sauce: Follow recipe for Medium White Sauce. Clean and slice ½ cup **mushrooms.** Heat 1 tablespoon **butter** in a skillet. Add the mushrooms and cook until lightly browned and tender. Mix into the cooked white sauce.

Breads

Scandinavians hold undisputed claim to being the greatest coffee drinkers in the world, and with their coffee they like a bit of sweet. Scandinavian homemakers have created coffee cakes and breads that are unrivaled for excellence. The wonderful Danish pastries and Swedish breads are perfect accompaniments for coffee. Dark breads, once a principal staple of diet, always accompany smörgåsbord or soup and form the base for open-face sandwiches.

Dilly Cottage Batter Bread

2½	cups all-purpose flour
1	package active dry yeast
1	tablespoon instant minced onion
1	teaspoon salt
½	teaspoon dill weed, thyme, or rosemary
1	cup creamed cottage cheese (at room temperature)
½	cup hot tap water (120° to 130°F)
1	egg (at room temperature)
1	tablespoon honey
1½	cups all-purpose flour

1. Combine 1 cup flour, yeast, onion, salt, and dill weed.
2. Add cottage cheese, water, egg, and honey to flour mixture; beat 3 minutes by hand or with electric mixer.
3. Beat in remaining flour. Cover; let rise in a warm place until double in bulk (about 1 hour).
4. Stir batter down; pour into a well-greased 1½-quart round casserole. Let rise in a warm place until light (30 to 40 minutes).
5. Bake at 375°F 50 to 55 minutes, or until done.

1 loaf

Danish Pastry

¾ **cup plus 2 tablespoons milk**

1 **pkg. active dry yeast**

¼ **cup warm water, 110°F to 115°F (Or if using compressed yeast, soften 1 cake in ¼ cup lukewarm water, 80°F to 85°F.)**

¼ **cup sugar**

¼ **cup butter**

¼ **teaspoon salt**

1 **cup sifted all-purpose flour**

2¼ **cups sifted all-purpose flour**

1 **egg, well beaten**

½ **cup butter**

½ **cup sugar**

½ **cup butter, cut in pieces**

½ **cup sifted confectioners' sugar**

1 **tablespoon milk**

1. Baking sheets will be needed.
2. Scald ¾ cup plus 2 tablespoons milk.
3. Meanwhile, soften yeast in water.
4. Set aside.
5. Put into a large bowl ¼ cup sugar, ¼ cup butter and salt.
6. Immediately pour scalded milk over ingredients in bowl. When likewarm, blend in 1 cup sifted all-purpose flour beating until smooth.
7. Stir softened yeast and add, mixing well.
8. Measure 2 to 2¼ cups sifted all-purpose flour.
9. Add about one-half the flour to the yeast mixture and beat until very smooth. Beat in egg.
10 Beat in enough remaining flour to make a soft dough. Cover with waxed paper and a towel and let stand in a warm place (about 80°F) until doubled.
11. Meanwhile, put into a bowl ½ cup of butter and ½ cup of sugar.
12. Set aside.
13. Set out ½ cup of butter, cut in pieces.
14. Turn dough onto a lightly floured surface. Roll into a rectangle 18x13 in. Using one third of the butter, cut in pieces, pat pieces down center third of dough. Cover butter with righthand third of dough. Fold left-hand third of dough under butter section. With rolling pin gently press down and seal open edges. Wrap in waxed paper. Chill in refrigerator 20 to 30 min.
15. Remove from refrigerator and place on board with butter section near top, narrow width toward you. Turn folded dough one-quarter way round to have open-under edge away from you. Roll to original size. Repeat two times the procedure for folding, sealing and chilling, using second and third portions of butter. Always place dough on floured surface.
16. Set out baking sheets.
17. After final chilling, roll dough to original size. Cut into 3-in. squares. Stir the sugar-butter mixture until blended. Place about 1½ teaspoons of the mixture in the center of each square. Fold the opposite corners in to center and press ends to seal. Place on the baking sheets. Cover with waxed paper and a towel. Let rise in a warm place until nearly doubled.
18. Bake at 450°F. 8 to 10 min.
19. Meanwhile, blend together confectioners' sugar and 1 tablespoon of milk.
20. When pastries are done, remove to cooling racks. Drizzle frosting over warm pastries. If desired, **preserves** may be substituted for the butter-sugar filling.

2 doz. pastries

Filled Coffee Cake

¼ **cup sifted all-purpose flour**

¾ **cup butter**

1 **pkg. active dry yeast**

¼ **cup warm water, 110°F to 115°F (Or if using compressed yeast, soften 1 cake in ¼ cup lukewarm water, 80°F to 85°F.)**

1 **egg**

¾ **cup milk**

3 **tablespoons sugar**

1 **teaspoon salt**

1 **cup sifted all-purpose flour**

2 **cups sifted all-purpose flour**

1½ **cups water**

1½ **cups (about ½ lb.) golden raisins**

¼ **cup butter**

1 **teaspoon cardamom**

2 **cups sifted confectioners' sugar**

3 **tablespoons cream**

⅓ **cup finely chopped blanched almonds**

Eggs lightly beaten

⅓ **cup sugar**

1. Baking sheets will be needed.
2. Measure ¼ cup sifted all-purpose flour.
3. Cut in ¾ cup butter with pastry blender or two knives until well blended.
4. Shape mixture into a ball and place on a long length of waxed paper. Cover with another long length of waxed paper and roll into a rectangle 10x4 in. Chill in refrigerator.
5. Meanwhile, soften the yeast in water.
6. Set aside.
7. Beat egg in a large bowl.
8. Beat in milk, 3 tablespoons of sugar and salt until sugar is dissolved.
9. Blend in 1 cup sifted all-purpose flour beating until smooth.
10. Stir softened yeast and add, mixing well.
11. Measure 2 cups sifted all-purpose flour.
12. Add about one-half the flour to the yeast mixture and beat until very smooth. Then beat in enough remaining flour to make a dough which leaves sides of bowl. Turn dough onto a lightly floured surface and roll into a 12-in. square.
13. Remove chilled flour-butter mixture from refrigerator, peel off waxed paper, and place in the center of the dough. Fold two sides of dough over flour-butter mixture so that sides overlap in center. Turn dough one-quarter way around and roll out again into a 12-in. square. Repeat the folding and rolling two more times, turning dough one-quarter way around each time. Wrap dough in waxed paper. Place in refrigerator to chill thoroughly, overnight if possible.
14. Meanwhile, bring water to boiling.
15. Add raisins and again bring to boiling.
16. Pour off water and drain raisins on absorbent paper. Set aside.
17. Cream, ¼ cup of butter and cardamon together until butter is softened.
18. Add confectioners' sugar gradually, beating thoroughly.
19. Blend in cream until the mixture is of spreading consistency.
20. Mix in the raisins and set aside.
21. Set out almonds.
22. Lightly grease two baking sheets.
23. Remove chilled dough from refrigerator and roll into a rectangle 24x12 in. Cut lengthwise with a sharp knife into two strips, 24x6 in. Spread each strip with one-half of the raisin filling. Starting with the long side of dough, roll up each strip tightly and pinch long edge to seal. Carefully stretch dough into a roll 30-in. long, being careful not to break dough.
24. Transfer rolls to the greased baking sheets. Form into pretzel shape by overlapping ends so that they touch long side of roll. Gently flatten dough to ½-in. thickness. Brush with egg.
25. Sprinkle with a mixture of the almonds and ⅓ cup sugar.
26. Cover with waxed paper and a clean towel. Let rise in a warm place (about 80°F.) until doubled.
27. Bake at 375°F. 20 to 25 min., or until lightly browned.

2 coffee cakes

Sweet Rye Bread I

2 pkgs. active dry yeast
½ cup warm water, 110°F to 115°F (Or if using compressed yeast, soften 1 cake in ½ cup lukewarm water, 80°F to 85°F.)
½ cup firmly packed brown sugar
⅓ cup molasses
1 tablespoon shortening
1 tablespoon salt
2 teaspoons caraway seed
½ teaspoon ground anise seed
1¼ cups hot water
5½ cups sifted all-purpose flour
2 cups rye flour

1. A baking sheet will be needed.
2. Soften the yeast in ½ cup warm water.
3. Set aside.
4. Meanwhile, put into a large bowl brown sugar, molasses, shortening, salt, caraway seed and anise seed.
5. Pour over ingredients in bowl 1¼ cups of hot water and set aside until lukewarm.
6. When lukewarm, blend in 1 cup sifted all-purpose flour beating until smooth.
7. Stir softened yeast and add mixing well.
8. Measure 4 to 4½ cups sifted all-purpose flour and rye flour.
9. Add the rye flour and beat until very smooth. Then beat in enough remaining flour to make a soft dough. Turn dough onto a very lightly floured surface. Allow dough to rest 5 to 10 min. Knead. Form dough into a large ball and put into a greased, deep bowl. Turn to bring greased surface to top. Cover with waxed paper and a towel and let stand in warm place (about 80°F) until dough is doubled.
10. Punch down with fist; pull edges in to center and turn dough completely over in bowl. Cover and let rise again until dough is nearly doubled.
11. Punch down dough and turn out on a lightly floured surface.
12. Grease the baking sheet.
13. Divide dough into two portions and shape into balls. Cover and allow to rest 5 to 10 min. Remove to greased baking sheet. Cover and let rise until dough is doubled.
14. Bake at 375°F. 25 to 35 min., or until lightly browned.
15. Cool completely on cooling racks.

2 loaves rye bread

Sweet Rye Bread II: Follow recipe for Sweet Rye Bread I. Put 1 tablespoon grated **orange peel** into the bowl with brown sugar.

Swedish Rye Bread: Follow recipe for Sweet Rye Bread I. Decrease brown sugar to ¼ cup and molasses to ¼

Swedish Tea Ring

1	cup milk or cream
1	pkg. active dry yeast
¼	cup warm water, 110°F to 115°F (Or if using compressed yeast, soften 1 cake in ¼ cup lukewarm water, 80°F to 85°F.)
½	cup sugar
1	teaspoon salt
5	cups sifted all-purpose flour
2	eggs, well beaten
¾	cup butter, softened
¾	cup firmly packed light brown sugar
1½	tablespoons cinnamon
½	cup (about 2½ oz.) dark seedless raisins
	Melted butter
½	cup sifted confectioners' sugar
1	tablespoon milk
½	teaspoon vanilla extract

1. Baking sheets will be needed.
2. Scald 1 cup of milk or cream.
3. Meanwhile, soften the yeast in warm water.
4. Set aside.
5. Put sugar and salt into a large bowl.
6. Pour scalded milk over ingredients in bowl.
7. When lukewarm, blend in 1 cup sifted all-purpose flour, beating until smooth.
8. Stir softened yeast and add, mixing well.
9. Measure 4 cups sifted all-purpose flour.
10. Add about one-half the flour to the yeast mixture and beat until very smooth. Beat in eggs.
11. Vigorously beat in ½ cup butter, 2 to 3 tablespoon at a time.
12. Beat in enough of the remaining flour to make a soft dough.
13. Turn dough onto a lightly floured surface. Allow dough to rest 5 to 10 min.
14. Knead. Form dough into a large ball and place it into a greased, deep bowl. Turn dough to bring greased surface to top. Cover with waxed paper and towel and let stand in warm place (about 80°F) until dough is doubled.
15. Punch down with fist; pull edges of dough in to center and turn dough completely over in bowl. Cover and let rise again unil nearly doubled.
16. Punch down and turn dough out onto lightly floured surface. Divide into two balls. Roll each ball into a rectangle 18x9-in.
17. Spread each rectangle with one-half of ¼ cup butter.
18. Sprinkle each rectangle with one-half of a mixture of brown sugar, cinnamon and raisins.
19. Beginning with the longer side, roll dough tightly. Press edges to seal.
20. Lightly grease two baking sheets.
21. Place uncut roll, sealed edge down, on the greased baking sheet. Pull ends together to form a ring, pressing slightly to seal ends. With scissors, snip at 1-in. intervals through ring almost to center. Turn each cut section on its side. Repeat procedure for the second ring. Brush rings lightly with melted butter.
22. Cover and let rise about 45 min., or until doubled.
23. Bake at 350°F. 20 to 25 min.
24. Meanwhile, blend together (for frosting) confectioners' sugar, 1 tablespoon milk and vanilla extract.
25. When tea rings are done, remove to cooling racks and frost while still warm.

2 tea rings

Coffee Bread

½ cup finely chopped blanched
  almonds
1 cup milk or cream
1 pkg. active dry yeast
¼ cup warm water, 110°F to
  115°F (Or if using com-
  pressed yeast, soften 1
  cake in ¼ cup lukewarm
  water, 80°F to 85°F.)
½ cup butter
⅓ cup sugar
1 teaspoon salt
1 cup sifted all-purpose
  flour
2½ cups sifted all-purpose
  flour
1 egg. well beaten
  Egg white, slightly beaten
⅓ cup sugar

1. Baking sheets will be needed.
2. Set out almonds.
3. Scald milk or cream.
4. Meanwhile, soften yeast in water.
5. Set aside.
6. Meanwhile, put butter, sugar and salt into a large bowl.
7. Immediately pour scalded milk over ingredients in bowl. When lukewarm, blend in 1 cup sifted all-purpose flour beating until smooth.
8. Stir softened yeast and add, mixing well.
9. Measure 2 to 2½ cups sifted all-purpose flour.
10. Add about one-half the flour to the yeast mixture and beat until very smooth.
11. Beat in egg.
12. Then beat in enough remaining flour to make a soft dough. Turn dough onto a lightly floured surface and allow dough to rest 5 to 10 min.
13. Knead. Form dough into a large ball and place it into a greased, deep bowl. Turn dough to bring greased surface to top. Cover with waxed paper and towel and let stand in warm place (about 80°F) until dough is doubled.
14. Punch down with fist; pull edges of dough in to center and turn dough completely over in bowl. Cover and let rise again until nearly doubled. Punch down and turn dough out onto lightly floured surface. Divide dough into two portions and shape into oblong loaves.
15. Lightly grease two baking sheets.
16. Place loaves onto baking sheets and brush with egg white.
17. Sprinkle each loaf with one half of a mixture of chopped almonds and ⅓ cup sugar.
18. Cover and let rise about 45 min., or until dough is doubled.
19. Bake at 375°F 20 to 25 min.
20. Cool completely on cooling racks.

2 loaves Coffee Bread

Cardamom Braid: Follow recipe for Coffee Bread. Add to ingredients in bowl 1 teaspoon **cardamon.** After second rising divide dough into 6 equal portions. Roll each portion into a strip about 1 in. thick. Place 3 strips on each greased baking sheet and braid tucking open ends under. Omit egg white and almond-sugar mixture. Cover and let rise about 45 min., or until doubled. Bake at 375°F about 25 min., or until lightly browned.

Saffron Braid: Follow recipe for Coffee Bread. Crumble very finely into a small cup enough saffron to yield 1 teaspoon **saffron.** Pour over the saffron 2 tablespoons boiling **water.** Stir and set aside to cool to lukewarm. Beat in with the egg. After second rising, divide dough into 6 equal portions. Roll each portion into a strip about 1-in. thick. Place 3 strips on each greased baking sheet and braid, tucking open ends under. Omit egg white and almond-sugar mixture. Cover and let rise about 45 min., or until doubled. Bake at 375°F about 25 min.

Twists: Follow recipe for Coffe Bread. Add to ingredients in bowl 1 tablespoon grated **orange peel.** Instead of dividing dough for loaves, break off pieces of dough and roll with hands into strips about 5 in. long and 3/8 in. thick. Shape as in Christmas Rolls. Or hold one end of strip and coil strip around finger, tucking end under securely. Or coil ends of strips in opposite directions until coils are opposite each other. Or coil strips as in Christmas Rolls but do not place two strips together. Press one **currant** firmly into the center of each coil. Place rolls on greased baking sheets. Omit egg white and almond-sugar mixture. Cover and let rise until doubled. Bake at 375°F 10 to 15 min.

About 4 doz. rolls

Christmas Rolls: Follow recipe for Coffee Bread. Instead of dividing dough for loaves, break off pieces of dough and roll with hands into strips 4 in. long and ½ in. thick. Coil each end in to center of strip. Place two coiled strips together so that coils are back to back. Or place two coiled strips at right angles, one on top of the other. Or shape strip into half circle and coil ends in opposite directions. Press one **raisin** into the center of each coil. Place rolls on greased baking sheets. Omit egg white and almond-sugar mixture. Cover and let rise until doubled. Bake at 375°F about 15 to 20 min.

About 4 doz. rolls

Lenten Buns

3 tablespons chopped blanched almonds

1 cup milk

1 pkg. active dry yeast

¼ cup warm water, 110°F to 115°F (Or if using compressed yeast, soften 1 cake in ¼ cup lukewarm water, 80°F to 85°F.)

½ cup butter

⅓ cup sugar

½ teaspoon salt

1 cup sifted all-purpose flour

3½ cups sifted all-purpose flour

2 eggs, well beaten

1½ cups sieved almond paste Vanilla Confectioners' Sugar (page 75)

½ cup chilled whipping cream

1. Baking sheets will be needed.
2. Set out almonds.
3. Scald milk.
4. Meanwhile, soften the yeast in water.
5. Set aside.
6. Put butter, sugar and salt into a large bowl.
7. Immediately pour scalded milk over ingredients in bowl. When lukewarm, blend in 1 cup sifted all-purpose flour beating until smooth.
8. Stir softened yeast and add mixing well.
9. Measure 2½ to 3½ cups sifted all-purpose flour.
10. Add about one-half the flour to the yeast mixture with the chopped almonds. Beat until very smooth.
11. Beat in eggs.
12. Then beat in enough remaining flour to make a soft dough. Turn dough onto a lightly floured surface and allow it to rest 5 to 10 min.
13. Knead. Form dough into a large ball and place it in a greased, deep bowl. Turn dough to bring greased surface to top. Cover with waxed paper and towel and let stand in warm place (about 80°F) until dough is doubled.
14. Punch down with fist; pull edges of dough in to center and turn dough completely over in bowl. Cover and let rise again until nearly doubled. Punch down and turn dough onto lightly floured surface.
15. Lightly grease the baking sheets.
16. Shape dough into 24 balls and place on the greased baking sheets. Cover and let rise about 45 min., or until doubled.
17. Bake at 425°F 15 to 20 min.
18. Cool buns completely on cooling racks.
19. Place a bowl and beater in refrigerator to chill.
20. Force enough almond paste through a sieve to yeild 1½ cups.
21. When buns are cool, cut a triangle ½ in. deep in the top of each. Carefully lift out triangular pieces. Spoon about 1 tablespoon of the almond paste into the cavity of each bun. Set pieces back on buns but without fitting to openings. Sprinkle buns lightly with vanilla confectioners' sugar.
22. Using the chilled bowl and beater, beat whipping cream until cream stands in peaks when beater is slowly lifted upright.
23. Force whipped cream through a pastry bag and a No. 27 star tube to decorate around center pieces.

2 doz. buns

Norwegian Christmas Bread

½ small orange
1 cup water
¾ cup (about 4 oz.) golden raisins
1 cup milk
1 pkg. active dry yeast
¼ cup warm water, 110°F to 115°F (Or if using compressed yeast, soften 1 cake in ¼ cup lukewarm water, 80°F to 85°F.)
½ cup butter
½ cup sugar
1 teaspoon salt
1 cup sifted all-purpose flour
1 teaspoon cardamom
3½ cups sifted all-purpose flour
Egg white, slightly beaten

1. A 9-in. round layer cake pan will be needed.
2. Rinse orange, cut into halves, remove any seeds and force through the medium blade of a food chopper.
3. Set aside.
4. Bring 1 cup water to boiling.
5. Add raisins and again bring to boiling.
6. Pour off water and drain raisins on absorbent paper. Set aside.
7. Scald milk.
8. Meanwhile, soften yeast in ¼ cup warm water.
9. Set aside.
10. Meanwhile, put butter, sugar and salt into a large bowl.
11. Immediately pour scalded milk over ingredients in bowl. When lukewarm, blend in 1 cup sifted all-purpose flour and cardamon, beating until smooth.
12. Stir softened yeast and add, mixing well.
13. Measure 3 to 3½ cups sifted all-purpose flour.
14. Add about one-half the flour to the yeast mixture and beat until very smooth.
15. Then beat in the ground orange, raisins, and enough remaining flour to make a soft dough. Turn dough onto a lightly floured surface and let rest 5 to 10 min.
16. Knead. Form dough into a large ball and place it into a greased, deep bowl. Turn dough to bring greased surface to top. Cover with waxed paper and towel and let stand in warm place (about 80°F) until dough is doubled.
17. Punch down with fist; pull edges of dough in to center and turn dough completely over in bowl. Cover and let rise again until nearly doubled. Punch down and turn dough out onto lightly floured surface.
18. Lightly grease the layer cake pan.
19. Shape the dough into a round ball, place in the greased pan and flatten slightly. Cover and let rise about 45 min., or until doubled.
20. Bake at 350°F 45 min. Remove from oven and brush with egg white.
21. Return to oven and bake 10 to 15 min. longer.
22. Remove bread from pan and place on cooling rack to cool completely.

1 loaf bread

Norwegian Potato Pancakes (Lefse)

6	medium-size (about 2 lbs.) potatoes, cut in halves
¼	cup butter
¼	cup milk
1½	teaspoon salt
1	teaspoon sugar
⅛	teaspoon pepper
3	cups sifted all-purpose flour
	Butter, softened

1. Wash potatoes, pare and cook.

2. Cook about 20 min., or until tender when pierced with a fork. Drain. To dry potatoes, shake pan over low heat.

3. Mash or rice potatoes thoroughly. Whip in ¼ cup butter and milk and a mixture of salt, sugar and pepper.

4. Whip potatoes until light and fluffy. Cool potatoes; chill in refrigerator.

5. Set a griddle or heavy skillet over low heat.

6. Measure flour.

7. Remove chilled potatoes from refrigerator. Add about one-half the flour and beat until smooth. Beat in enough remaining flour to make a soft dough. Shape dough into a ball and turn on-to a lightly floured surface. Roll into a round about 1/8 in. thick. Cut into 6-in. rounds.

8. Test griddle by dropping on it a few drops cold water; if drops dance around in small beads, griddle temperature is right. Do not grease the griddle.

9. Place Lefse on griddle and cook until lightly browned. Turn and lightly brown other side. Then turning frequently, continue cooking until Lefse are browned and dry. Remove to a clean dry towel. Cool Lefse completely.

10. Spread cold Lefse with butter.

11. Roll loosely and serve.

About 2½ doz. Lefse

Danish Sandwiches

Danish smørrebrød are open-faced sandwiches. Their genealogy is not known, but sometime early in the nineteenth century, the smørrebrød became a reigning favorite of the Danish menu and it has maintained this position to the present. At least once a day and sometimes oftener, practically all the Danes in Denmark are enthusiastically preparing, serving, eating and enjoying the renowned open-faced sandwich. Restaurants take pride in the variety they offer and the menus for these sandwiches can run along for a yard or more—like a proud banner. Indeed, the smørrebrød is a custom that foreign visitors joyfully support on trips to the smallest of the Scandinavian countries and remember longingly after they leave.

Virtually all of the produce of land and sea lends itself in some way to the enchantment of the open sandwich, but combinations are not haphazard or merely daring. They are artfully and wisely selected for the perfect mating of flavors. Garnishes and sauces must not mask flavors but accent and enhance them, and by the strictest standards each sandwich must be an object of visual beauty as well as gastronomic appeal. This interesting culinary art has a dual mission: to delight at the same time that it nourishes. Sandwiches may be entertaining, but always within the bounds of good taste—in both meanings of that phrase.

The base of these famed sandwich creations is a single slice of bread, the type depending on what is to compose the sandwich. Danish preference runs to the rye breads. White bread, if it is used, is usually toasted. The kind and amount of butter is also determined by the other ingredients, as are the sauces, garnishes and seasonings. And what then composes the spreads? Virtually anything.

Foremost in popular favor is a sandwich that consists of one slice of lightly buttered **bread** heaped with the prized Danish June **shrimp** or covered with the pink beauties in a pattern so tight that it resembles fish scales. A cleaned crisp **lettuce leaf** garnishes this creation. Seasonings for so prized a delicacy are considered superfluous; later in the season, when the shrimp run larger and coarser, **mayonnaise** may be added—and a whisper of **curry.**

In another seafood sandwich **lobster meat**—fresh or canned—is sliced onto bread over a spread of **butter** or **mayonnaise.** Sometimes a ribbon of mayonnaise is run across the lobster and an accent of minced **dill** may be added.

Herring in almost all of its forms—**marinated, spiced** and **kippered**—is lavishly used for open sandwiches but rarely combined with anything more than the **onion rings** for which herring seems to have a special affinity. Sometimes a raw **egg yolk,** held in place with a ring of onion, accompanies the herring sandwich, and sliced **hard-cooked egg** is also acceptable.

There are literally hundreds of other kinds of open sandwiches. A sampling of the better-known varieties would include: **ham,** beautifully garnished with chopped cooked **spinach, mushrooms** and grilled **tomato;** panbroiled **bacon,** sliced **tomatoes, liver paste, jellied meat** and freshly grated **horseradish;** soft **cheese** with a sprinkling of minced **radish** or **celery;** sliced **smoked salmon** on a bed of **scrambled eggs; liver sausage** on finely sliced tart **apple; chopped ham** with raw **egg yolk** and a bit of chopped **chives; roast pork slices** with a **lettuce cup** of cucumber, **pickled beets** or **cabbage relish;** scraped **raw beef** with **smoked salmon** and **caviar** or with a couple of **oysters,** a ribbon of **caviar** and a few **shrimp; ham** and **beef slices** with a **lettuce cup** of **mustard pickle; sardines** on a bed of sliced **cucumbers** with a ribbon of chopped **radishes** and sieved **hard-cooked eggs;** sliced **tongue** with **macaroni salad; lobster** and cooked **asparagus pieces** tossed with **mayonnaise** and laid over a **lettuce leaf; herring salad** with a decoration of sliced **hard-cooked egg** or a **fried egg,** sunny-side up; thrifty slices of cold boiled **potato** on salami with a ribbon of chopped **chives.**

If Danish sandwiches are to live up to their well-earned reputation a few principles must be observed in making them. They must be prepared immediately or shortly before they are served. Bread must never be soggy; if ingredients are dampish the serviceable lettuce leaf may be used as a shield for the bread. **Seasoned butters** may of course be used but should be carefully chosen to match or pleasantly contrast with other flavors.

Cakes and Desserts

The dessert traditions of Scandinavia differ from our own in several ways. Pies are unknown and the torte and a sponge-type cake are more popular than our frosted layer cakes. Fruit soups are often served for dessert, and clabbered milk and puddings abound—especially rum, almond, fruit, and rice puddings. In Sweden tiny thin pancakes, baked in a special platt pan and served with fruit preserves or syrups, have a universal following. Fresh fruits, particularly the luscious berries of Scandinavia, are popular summertime desserts. They are served at the peak of their flavor and unadorned—except for rich cream and sugar.

Swedish Applecake with Vanilla Sauce

Vanilla Sauce (page 66)
16 (about 7 oz.) rusks
¼ cup sugar
⅓ cup butter
2½ cups thick sweetened applesauce
¼ cup butter
¼ cup sifted confectioners' sugar

1. Butter bottom and sides of a 1-qt. baking dish.
2. Prepare vanilla sauce.
3. Place rusks on a long length of heavy waxed paper.
4. Loosely fold paper around rusks, tucking under open ends. With a rolling pin, gently crush rusks to make fine crumbs (about 2 cups crumbs). Or place rusks in a plastic bag and gently crush. Turn crumbs into a bowl. Stir in sugar.
5. Melt cup butter in a saucepan over low heat.
6. Pour butter evenly over the crumb mixture and toss lightly to coat crumbs evenly.
7. Put one-third of the crumbs into the baking dish and firmly press into an even layer on bottom and sides of baking dish.
8. Set out applesauce and ¼ cup butter.
9. Spoon one-half the applesauce into the baking dish. Dot with one-half of the butter. Sprinkle with one-half the remaining crumbs. Repeat layering, ending with remaining crumbs.
10. Bake at 350°F 25 to 30 min.
11. Cool completely; chill in refrigerator several hours.
12. When ready to serve, sift confectioners' sugar over top of cake to form a decorative pattern*.
13. Serve applecake with the Vanilla Sauce.

8 servings

*Note: To form a pattern place a paper doily on top of the cake. Sift the confectioners' sugar over the doily. Carefully lift doily off the cake. The confectioners' sugar will form the decorative pattern.

Coffee Torte

2 cups (about ½ lb.) pecans (about 3½ cups, grated)
3 tablespoons concentrated soluble coffee
7 egg yolks
1 cup sugar
7 egg whites
⅛ teaspoon salt
Mocha Mallow Whipped Cream Fosting (page 65)

1. Set out two 9-in. round layer cake pans. Grease pans (bottom and sides) and line bottoms with waxed paper. Grease waxed paper. Cut two lengths of parchment paper 2-in. wide and 30 in. long. Line sides of pans with the parchment paper, pressing paper against sides of pans. Fasten ends with cellulose tape.
2. Grate pecans.
3. Thouroughly combine coffee with pecans.
4. Divide into four portions by marking with a spatula. Set aside.
5. Beat yolk and sugar until very thick and lemon colored.
6. Set egg-yolk mixture aside.
7. Beat egg whites and salt until rounded peaks are formed and egg whites do not slide when bowl is partially inverted.
8. Gently spread egg-yolk mixture over beaten egg whites. Spoon one portion of the pecan-coffee mixture over egg mixture and gently fold with a few strokes until batter is only partially blended. Repeat with second and third portions. Spoon remaining fourth of pecan-coffee mixture over batter and gently fold just until blended. Do not overmix! Gently turn batter into pans and spread to edges.
9. Bake at 350°F 25 to 30 min., or until torte test done.
10. Cool; remove from pans as directed.
11. When torte is cooled, prepare Mocha Mallow Whipped Cream frosting.
12. Fill and frost and place in refrigerator until ready to serve.

12 to 16 servings

Hazelnut Torte

1 cup (about 4¾ oz.) hazelnuts (about 1¾ cups, grated)
2 tablespoons sifted all-purpose flour
2 teaspoons baking powder
3 eggs
¾ cup sugar
¼ cup sifted confectioners' sugar

1. Set out two 8-in. round layer cake pans.
2. Grate hazelnuts.
3. Sift together flour and baking powder.
4. Blend flour mixture and grated nuts together and set aside.
5. Beat eggs until thick and piled softly.
6. Gradually blend in sugar.
7. Gently fold nut-flour mixture into the egg mixture. Turn batter into the pans.
8. Bake at 350°F 20 min., or until torte tests done. Invert pans and let layers hang until cool. (If torte is higher than pan, invert between two cooling racks so that top of torte does not touch any surface.)
9. When torte is cooled, remove from pans as directed. Sift confectioners' sugar over tops of layers.
10. Cut into wedges before serving.

12 to 16 servings

Filled Hazelnut Torte: Follow recipe for Hazelnut Torte. Prepare **Sweetened Whipped Cream** (use 1 cup chilled whipping cream). Fill the torte with the whipped cream. Sprinkle top of torte with **confectioners' sugar.**

Almond Cake

1½	cups sifted all-purpose flour
½	cup sugar
1	teaspoon baking powder
½	cup butter
1	egg, beaten
⅔	cup (about 3 oz.) blanched almonds
⅔	cup sifted confectioners' sugar
1	egg, beaten

1. Set out an 8-in. round layer cake pan.
2. Sift together flour, sugar and baking powder into a bowl.
3. Cut in butter with a pastry blender or two knives until well blended.
4. Blend 1 egg in thoroughly.
5. Chill dough in refrigerator.
6. Meanwhile, grate almonds.
7. Thoroughly mix with almonds ⅔ cup sifted confectioners' sugar.
8. Blend in 1 beaten egg.
9. Remove chilled dough from refrigerator and divide into two balls. Put one ball in the cake pan and return remaining ball to refrigerator. Using hands, work dough in pan to cover bottom and sides. Turn almond mixture into the cake pan, spreading evenly over surface of dough. Remove dough from refrigerator. Cut off pices of dough and roll with hands into rolls about ½ to ¾ in. thick. Arrange four strips parallel to each other across filling. Arrange four strips at right angles, weaving over and under to form a lattice. Roll remaining dough into a thin roll and arrange round edge of cake, pressing ends together to seal. If dough becomes too sticky to handle, return to refrigerator for about 10 min.
10. Bake at 375°F 25 to 30 min., or until lightly browned.
11. Set on a cooling rack to cool completely. With a spatula, loosen sides of cake from pan and cut into wedges. Or loosen sides of cake from pan and carefully remove cake from pan.

6 to 8 servings

Apple Torte

1¼	cups sifted all-purpose flour
1	cup butter, softened
6	tablespoons sifted all-purpose flour
½	lb. (about 2 cups) dried apples
3	cups water
1	cup sugar
¾	teaspoon cinnamon
½	cup (about 2 oz.) blanched almonds, split in half

1. Set out a 9-in. pie pan.
2. Measure 1¼ cups sifted all-purpose flour, into a bowl.
3. Cut in ½ cup butter with pastry blender or two knives until blended.
4. Cover and set aside overnight (in a cool place but not in refrigerator).
5. The next day, cut in ½ cup butter with a pastry blender or two knives until well blended.
6. Add and blend thoroughly 6 tablespoons sifted all purpose flour.
7. Chill in refrigerator.
8. Put apples and water into a 3-qt. heavy saucepan.
9. Cook over medium heat 30 min. Stir in ¾ cup sugar and cinnamon.
10. Cook 15 min. longer. Cool completely.
11. Remove pastry from refrigerator. Divide into two balls. Set each ball on a length of waxed paper. Cover with another length of waxed paper. Roll from center to edge into a round about 1/8 in. thick and about 1 in. larger than overall size of pan. Chill in refrigerator.
12. Set out almonds.
13. When pastry is chilled, remove a layer from refrigerator and peel off waxed paper. Place pastry in pie pan and press evenly

over bottom and sides of pan. Turn the apple mixture into the pie pan. Remove the second pastry layer from refrigerator and place on top of apple mixture. Gently press edges to seal. Fold extra pastry under bottom pastry. Flute or press edges together with a fork. With the tines of a fork pierce top in several places. Arrange the almond halves in a decorative pattern over top of torte.

14. Sprinkle ¼ cup sugar evenly over top of torte.

15. BAke at 375°F 45 to 50 min., or until browned.

16. Cool completely on cooling rack. To serve, cut into wedges.

6 to 8 servings

Mazarin Cake

Raspberry Sauce (page 66)
¾ **cup sifted all-purpose flour**
¾ **cup butter**
¼ **cup sugar**
1 **egg yolk, slightly beaten**
½ **lb. (about 1½ cups) blanched almonds**
⅓ **cup sifted confectioners' sugar**
4 **egg yolks, well beaten**
¼ **cup sifted confectioners' sugar**
1½ **teaspoon milk**

1. Lightly butter an 8-in. cake pan with removable bottom.

2. Prepare and chill raspberry sauce in refrigerator.

3. For Pastry—Measure flour and set aside.

4. Cream ¼ cup butter until softened.

5. Add sugar gradually, creaming until fluffy after each addition.

6. Blend in 1 egg yolk.

7. Add the flour in halves, blending well after each addition. Chill pastry in refrigerator.

8. For Filling—Meanwhile, grate almonds.

9. Blend in confectioners' sugar.

10. Set aside.

11. Cream ½ cup butter until softened.

12. Blend in 4 eggs yolks.

13. Blend in the almond-sugar mixture until smooth. Set filling aside.

14. To Complete Cake—Remove pastry from the refrigerator and place on a lightly floured surface. Roll ¼ in. thick and about 1 in. larger than overall size of pan. With knife or spatula, loosen pastry from surface wherever sticking occurs; lift pastry slightly and sprinkle flour underneath.

15. With spatula, loosen pastry and fold in half and then in quarters. Gently lay pastry in pan and unfold, fitting it to the pan so that it is not stretched.

16. Trim edge with scissors or sharp knife, leaving ½ in. overlap. Fold extra pastry under at edge and flute or press edges together with a fork. Spread the Raspberry Sauce evenly over the pastry at bottom of pan. Carefully spread almond mixture over the Raspberry Sauce being careful to cover sauce completely.

17. Bake at 325°F 35 to 40 min., or until lightly browned.

18. Cool completely on a cooling rack.

19. Meanwhile, blend together confectioners' sugar and milk.

20. When ready to serve, carefully remove cake from pan to cake plate. Spread confectioners' sugar glaze over top of cake. Or omit glaze and sprinkle cake with confectioners' sugar.

One 8-in. cake.

Sugar Cake

1½	cups sifted all-purpose flour
2	teaspoons baking powder
⅛	teaspoon salt
½	cup boiling water
¼	cup butter
3	eggs
1	cup less 1 tablespoon sugar
2	teaspoons grated lemon peel
	Vanilla Confectioners' Sugar (page 75)

1. Butter a 2-qt. fancy tubed mold or a form cake mold.
2. Sift together flour, baking powder and salt and set aside.
3. Measure water.
4. Add butter to the water and set aside to cool.
5. Beat eggs until very thick and piled softly.
6. Add sugar gradually, beating thoroughly after each addition.
7. Stir in lemon peel.
8. Sift dry ingredients over mixture, about one-fourth at a time; gently fold until just blended after each addition. Add the water-butter mixture all at one time and quickly mix just until smooth. Turn into the prepared pan.
9. Bake at 325°F 1 hr., or until cake tests done.
10. Cool completely; run a small sharp knife around tube and sides; remove cake from pan.
11. Sprinkle cake generously with vanilla confectioners' sugar.
12. Or serve plain with fruit or ice cream.

One tubed cake

Danish Rum Pudding I

¼	cup cold water
2	teaspoons unflavored gelatin
4	egg yolks, slightly beaten
2	cups heavy cream
½	cup sugar
¼	teaspoon salt
3	tablespoons rum
	Lingonberries or Raspberry Sauce (page 66)

1. Set out 6 custard cups.
2. Pour water into a small cup or custard cup.
3. Sprinkle gelatin evenly over cold water.
4. Set aside.
5. Blend egg yolks, cream, sugar and salt well in top of double boiler.
6. Cook over simmering water, stirring constantly and rapidly, until egg-yolk mixture coats a silver spoon.
7. Remove from heat and strain into a bowl. Immediately blend in softened gelatin, stirring until gelatin is completely dissolved. Set aside to cool, stirring occasionally.
8. Add and stir rum until thoroughly blended.
9. Pour mixture into the custard cups and set in refrigerator to chill (about 2 hrs).
10. When ready to serve, unmold desserts by carefully running a knife around inside edges of cups; invert onto serving dishes.
11. Serve with lingonberries or raspberry sauce.

6 servings

Note: For a more delicate gel, use only 1 teaspoon of gelatin.

Danish Rum Pudding II

½ cup cold water
1½ tablespoons unflavored gelatin
6 egg yolks
1 cup sugar
6 tablespoons rum
2 tablespoons lemon juice
6 egg whites
Sweetened whipped cream
Sweetened whole strawberries
Raspberry Sauce (page 66)

1. Set out a 2½-qt. fancy mold.
2. Pour water into a small saucepan.
3. Sprinkle gelatin evenly over water.
4. Set saucepan over low heat and stir constantly until gelatin is completely dissolved. Remove from heat.
5. Beat egg yolks until thick and lemon colored.
6. Add sugar gradually, beating thoroughly.
7. Mix in rum and lemon juice.
8. Stir the dissolved gelatin and blend into the egg mixture.
9. Beat eggs whites until rounded peaks are formed and egg whites do not slide when bowl is partially inverted.
10. Spread egg-yolk mixture over beaten egg whites. Gently but thoroughly fold together. Rinse the mold with cold water. Turn mixture into the mold and set in refrigerator to chill until firm.
11. When ready to serve, unmold onto a chilled serving plate. Garnish with sweetened whipped cream.
12. Arrange strawberries around the pudding.
13. Serve with raspberry sauce.

8 to 10 servings

Danish Rum Pudding III

½ cup cold water
2 env. unflavored gelatin
6 egg yolks
½ cup sugar
2 cups milk
½ cup cream
6 tablespoons rum
6 egg whites
Raspberry Sauce (page 66) or Lingonberry preserves

1. Set out a 2½-qt. mold.
2. Pour water into a small bowl.
3. Sprinkle gelatin evenly over cold water.
4. Set aside.
5. Beat egg yolks with rotary or electric beater until thick and lemon-colored.
6. Add sugar gradually, beating constantly.
7. Add milk and cream gradually to egg-yolk mixture, stirring until well blended.
8. Pour into top of double boiler and place over simmering water. Cook, stirring constantly, until mixture coats a silver spoon. Remove top of double boiler from heat and simmering water. Immediately stir in softened gelatin until gelatin is completely dissolved.
9. Chill in refrigerator or pan of ice and water until mixture begins to gel (gets slightly thicker). (If placed over ice and water, stir frequently; if placed in refrigerator, stir occasionally.)
10. Blend in rum.
11. Beat egg whites until rounded peaks are formed.
12. Spread beaten egg whites over mixture and gently fold together. Rinse mold in cold water. Turn mixture into the mold. Chill in refrigerator until firm.
13. When ready to serve, unmold onto a chilled serving plate and serve with raspberry sauce or lingonberry preserves.

10 to 12 servings

Swedish Christmas Porridge

6 cups milk
1 cup rice
3 tablespoons sugar
½ teaspoon salt
1 whole blanched almond
Cool milk
Sugar
Cinnamon

1. Put 6 cups milk, rice, 3 tablespoon sugar and salt into the top of a double boiler. (The Rice Industry no longer considers it necessary to wash rice before cooking.)
2. Cover and cook over simmering water 2½ to 3 hrs., or until rice is entirely soft when a kernel is pressed between fingers and mixture is quite thick. Remove cover for last 10 min. if mixture is not thick enough.
3. Mix in almond just before serving.
4. Serve with cool milk, sugar and cinnamon.
5. Or serve with a fruit sauce.

6 servings

Caramel Pudding

½ cup sugar
2 cups heavy cream
3 eggs
¼ cup sugar
1 teaspoon vanilla extract
Whole blanched almonds

1. Set out a 1-qt. baking dish.
2. Put ½ cup sugar into a heavy skillet over medium heat.
3. With back of a wooden spoon keep sugar moving constantly in skillet until sugar is completely melted, and of a rich medium brown color (caramelized). Pour caramelized sugar into the baking dish. Quickly tilt baking dish until bottom is evenly coated. Set aside.
4. Heat water for hot water bath.
5. Scald cream.
6. Meanwhile, beat eggs slightly.
7. Mix in ¼ cup sugar.
8. Stirring constantly, gradually add hot cream to the egg mixture. Stir until sugar is dissolved. Blend in vanilla extract.
9. Strain mixture into the baking dish.
10. Bake uncovered in the hot water bath at 325°F 55 to 60 min., or until silver knife comes out clean when inserted halfway between center and edge of baking dish. Remove carefully from the hot water bath. Set on a cooling rack until lukewarm. Chill pudding thoroughly in refrigerator.
11. When ready to serve, unmold by running a knife around inside edge of baking dish; invert onto a chilled serving dish. Garnish with whole blanched almonds.
12. Top of mold will be caramel-coated and excess coating will run down sides of mold to form a sauce at base of pudding.

6 servings

Individual Caramel Puddings: Follow recipe for Caramel Pudding. Set out 6 custard cups. Reduce sugar to ⅓ cup. Pour some of the caramelized sugar into each custard cup. Bake puddings 40 to 45 min.

Snow Pudding

Vanilla Sauce (page 66)
2 **env. unflavored gelatin**
1¼ **cups sugar**
⅛ **teaspoon salt**
2½ **cups water**
⅓ **cup strained lemon juice**
6 **egg whites**

1. Prepare vanilla sauce.
2. Mix gelatin, sugar and salt thoroughly in a saucepan.
3. Stir in water.
4. Set the saucepan over low heat and stir constantly until gelatin and sugar are completely dissolved. Remove the saucepan from heat. Mix in lemon juice.
5. Chill in refrigerator or in a pan of ice and water until mixture is slightly thicker than consistency of thick unbeaten egg white. (If mixture is placed over ice and water, stir frequently; if placed in refrigerator, stir occasionally.)
6. Lightly oil a 2½-qt. fancy mold with salad or cooking oil (not olive oil). Invert the mold and set it aside to drain.
7. When gelatin is of desired consistency, beat egg whites until rounded peaks are formed and egg whites do not slide when bowl is partially inverted.
8. Beat gelatin mixture with a rotary or electric beater until frothy. Gently but thoroughly fold gelatin mixture into beaten egg whites. Turn into prepared mold. Chill in refrigerator until firm (at least 4 hrs.)
9. When ready to serve, unmold onto chilled serving plate.
10. Serve with Vanilla Sauce.

8 to 10 servings

Sour Cream Waffles

¼ **cup butter**
1 **cup sifted all-purpose flour**
2 **tablespoons sugar**
1 **teaspoon baking soda**
1 **teaspoon cardamom**
½ **teaspoon salt**
2 **egg yolks**
1 **cup thick sour cream**
1 **cup buttermilk**
2 **egg whites**
Butter

1. Heat waffle baker while preparing waffle batter.
2. Melt butter and set aside to cool.
3. Sift together flour, sugar, baking soda, cardamom and salt into a large bowl.
4. Set aside.
5. Beat egg yolks until thick and lemon-colored.
6. Add the melted butter, sour cream and buttermilk gradually.
7. Continue to beat until well blended. Add liquid mixture all at one time to dry ingredients; mix only until batter is smooth.
8. Beat egg whites until rounded peaks are formed.
9. Spread the beaten egg whites over the batter and gently fold together.
10. Unless temperature is automatically shown on waffle baker, test baker; it is hot enough for baking when drops of water sprinkled on surface "sputter." Pour batter into center of waffle baker. It is wise to experiment to find out the exact amount of batter your baker will hold; use that same measurement (spoonfuls or cupfuls) in future waffle baking.
11. Lower cover and allow waffle to bake according to manufacturer's directions, or until steaming stops (about 5 min.). Do not raise cover during baking period. Lift cover and loosen waffle with a fork. Set waffles aside on a clean towel. As each waffle is baked pile on previous waffles to keep soft.
12. Serve waffles cold. Spread with butter.
13. If desired, serve with lingonberry preserves or jam.

About 4 waffles

Swedish Pancakes

1½ **cups sifted all-purpose flour**
3 **tablespoons sugar**
½ **teaspoon salt**
3 **eggs**
2 **cups milk**
2 **tablespoons melted butter**
Butter
Lingonberry preserves

1. Set out a griddle or large, heavy skillet. A Swedish platt pan (available at most department stores) may be used for these pancakes.
2. Sift together flour, sugar, and salt into a large bowl and set aside.
3. Beat eggs in a bowl until thick and piled softly.
4. Beat in milk and 2 tablespoons melted butter until blended.
5. Add to dry ingredients and beat until smooth.
6. Heat griddle over low heat; it is hot enough when drops of water sprinkled on surface dance in small beads. Lightly grease with butter.
7. For each pancake spoon about 1 tablespoon batter onto griddle or skillet (pancakes should be about 2½ to 3 in. in diameter). Cook each pancake over medium heat until lightly browned on bottom. Loosen edges with a spatula, turn, and lightly brown second side. As each pancake is cooked, transfer to a heated plate. Arrange pancakes in a circle, slightly overlapping each other. In center, set a bowl of lingonberry preserves.

5 doz. 3-in. pancakes.

Apple Pancake Cake: Follow recipe for Swedish Pancakes. Prepare six 8-in. pancakes. As each pancake is cooked, transfer it to a platter; spread with ¼ cup thick, sweetened **applesauce.** Do not spread applesauce on top pancake. (Remaining batter may be used for plattar.) Chill. Prepare **Sweetened Whipped Cream** (use 1 cup chilled **whipping cream**). Frost pancake stack with cream. Chill in refrigerator until ready to serve. Cut into wedges.

6 to 8 servings

Mocha Mallow Whipped Cream Frosting

2 **cups whipping cream**
16 **(4 oz.) marshmallows**
⅓ **cup coffee beverage (page 76; use 4 teaspoons concentrated soluble coffee)**

1. Set in refrigerator a bowl, rotary beater and whipping cream.
2. Heat together marshmallows and coffee beverage in top of double boiler over simmering water, stirring occasionally, until marshmallows are melted.
3. Remove from heat. Cool; chill in refrigerator.
4. When mixture is chilled, whip the cream, using the chilled bowl and beater. Whip 1 cup at a time until cream is of medium consistency (piles softly). Fold whipped cream into chilled mixture.

Enough to fill and frost one 9-in. torte

Pancake Balls

2	cups sifted all-purpose flour
2	tablespoons sugar
1	teaspoon baking soda
1	teaspoon cardamom
¾	teaspoon salt
1	cup thick sour cream
⅔	cup milk
3	egg yolks, beaten
2	tablespoons melted butter
3	egg whites
	Butter (about ½ teaspoon per well)
	Confectioners' sugar

1. Set an ableskiver pan (available in the housewares section of most department stores) over low heat.
2. Sift together flour, sugar, baking soda, cardamom and salt and set aside.
3. Combine sour cream, milk, egg yolks and butter.
4. Make a well in center of dry ingredients. Add liquid mixture all at one time, stirring until well blended.
5. Beat egg whites until rouded peaks are formed.
6. Gently spread batter over egg whites and fold together.
7. Test ableskiver pan by dropping on it a few drops cold water; if drops dance around in small beads, temperature is right. Grease wells with butter (about ½ teaspoon per well).
8. Pour batter into wells, filling about one half full. With a fork turn ableskivers frequently to brown evenly. Do not pierce. Ableskivers are done when a wooden pick inserted in center comes out clean.
9. Serve immediately sprinkled with confectioners' sugar.
10. If desired, accompany with a tart jam.

About 4 doz. balls.

Apple Pancake Balls: Follow recipe for Pancake Balls. Rinse, pare and dice 2 medium-size **apples.** Sprinkle about 1 teaspoon of the diced apples over batter in each well.

Cream Filling

1	cup milk
⅓	cup sugar
2	tablespoons all-purpose flour
⅛	teaspoon salt
2	egg yolks, slightly beaten
1	tablespoon butter
1	teaspoon vanilla extract

1. Measure milk.
2. Scald ¾ cup of the milk.
3. Meanwhile, sift together sugar, flour and salt into a saucepan.
4. Add, stirring well the remaining ¼ cup cold milk. Add gradually, stirring in, scalded milk. Wash double boiler top to remove scum.
5. Stirring gently and constantly, bring flour mixture rapidly to boiling over direct heat and boil 3 min. Pour into double boiler top and place over simmering water. Cover and cook about 5 to 7 min., stirring occasionally.
6. Vigorously stir about 3 tablespoons of the hot mixture into egg yolks.
7. Immediately blend into mixture in double boiler. Cook over simmering water 3 to 5 min. Stir slowly to keep mixture cooking evenly.
8. Remove from heat. Stir in butter and vanilla extract.
9. Cover and set filling aside to cool slightly, stirring occasionally; set in refrigerator to chill.

About 1 cup filling

Raspberry Sauce

2	cups fresh raspberries
½	cup sugar
1	tablespoon cold water
1½	teaspoons cornstarch

1. Set out a heavy 1-qt. saucepan.
2. Sort, rinse and thoroughly drain raspberries.
3. Force berries through a sieve or food mill into the saucepan. Blend in sugar.
4. Set berry mixture aside.
5. Blend together water and cornstarch to make a smooth paste.
6. Thoroughly blend into berry mixture. Stirring gently and constantly, bring rapidly to boiling. Continue stirring and boil over medium heat about 3 min. Set aside to cool. Store in refrigerator.

About 1 cup sauce

Vanilla Sauce

⅓	cup butter
½	cup sugar
6	egg yolks, slightly beaten
¾	cup boiling water
1	teaspoon vanilla extract

1. Cream butter until is softened.
2. Add sugar gradually, creaming until fluffy after each addition.
3. Add egg yolks gradually, blending in.
4. Add water very gradually.
5. Put mixture in top of double boiler and cook over simmering water, stirring constantly, until thickened.
6. Remove from heat and blend in vanilla extract.
7. Cool; chill in refrigerator.

About 2 cups sauce

Peach Sherbet

¾	lb. well-ripened peaches
½	bottle white wine
8	oz. water
4	oz. sugar
	juice of 1 lemon
½	cup heavy cream
2	ripe peaches, sliced

1. Bring water and sugar to a boil and let boil for a couple of minutes.
2. Remove pits from peaches and cut fruit in thin slices. Place in a large bowl. Pour warm sugared water over peach slices and let cool. Add wine. Let stand overnight.
3. Strain peaches and mix or puree with wine and syrup in a blender. Add lemon juice.
4. Place bowl in freezer for 1 hour or until it starts to set. Remove from freezer at half hour intervals for three hours and beat rapidly each time.
5. Serve frozen sherbet immediately after last whipping in large wine glasses.
Top with whipped cream and fresh peach slices.

8 servings.

Cookies

The cookie jars of Scandinavia are usually full, and they are always crammed to bursting for the Christmas holidays. Because butter is used with unstinting hand, the cookies meet the tongue meltingly. They keep well in tightly covered containers. Almond is a favorite flavoring. Salt is rarely used in Scandinavian cookies.

Finnish Coffee Fingers

½   **cup very finely chopped blanched almonds**
3   **tablespoons sugar**
1¼   **cups sifted all-purpose flour**
½   **cup butter**
1   **teaspoon almond extract**
2   **tablespoons sugar**
    Egg white, slightly beaten

1. Set out cookie sheets.
2. Set out mixture of almonds and 3 tablespoons sugar.
3. Measure flour and set aside.
4. Cream together butter and almond extract until butter is softened.
5. Add 2 tablespoons sugar gradually, creaming until fluffy after each addition.
6. Add the flour in fourths, thoroughly blending in after each addition. Chill in refrigerator.
7. Cut off small pieces of chilled dough and roll with the hands about ¼ in. thick and 2½ in. long to resemble fingers. Brush cookies with egg white.
8. Roll fingers in the almond mixture. Carefully place cookies on the cookie sheets.
9. Bake at 350°F 10 to 12 min., or until cookies are golden yellow.
10. With a spatula, carefully remove cookies to cooling racks to cool completely.

About 5 doz. cookies

Spritz Cookies

2½ cups sifted all-purpose flour
1 cup butter
1 teaspoon vanilla extract
½ cup sugar
2 egg yolks

1. Set out cookie sheets.
2. Measure flour and set aside.
3. Cream together butter and vanilla extract until butter is softened.
4. Add sugar gradually, creaming until fluffy after each addition.
5. Thoroughly beat in egg yolks one at a time.
6. Add flour in fourths, thoroughly blending in after each addition.
7. Fill a cookie press about two-thirds full with dough. According to manufacturer's directions, form cookies of varied shapes directly onto cookie sheets.
8. Bake at 350°F 12 to 15 min., or until cookies are golden yellow.
9. With spatula, carefully remove cookies to cooling racks; cool completely.

About 6 doz. cookies

For Variety: *Jelly:* before baking made a small depression at center of some round cookies and spoon ¼ to ½ teaspoon **jelly** onto centers of cookies. *Nuts:* lightly brush slightly beaten egg white over unbaked cookies and sprinkle each with about ½ teaspoon finely chopped **pistachios.** *Confectioners' Sugar:* lightly sift **confectioners' sugar** over baked and cooled cookies. *Maraschino Cherries:* press ¼ **maraschino cherry** onto center of round cookies before baking. *Colored Sugar:* lightly sprinkle unbaked cookies with red or green **colored sugar.** *Chocolate-Dipped:* partially melt over simmering water candy-making **chocolate** for dipping or semi-sweet chocolate pieces. Remove from heat and stir until it is melted. Stir in **butter** (1 tablespoon butter for 2 oz. chocolate) until butter is melted and blended in. Immediately coat ends of some cookies by dipping in chocolate mixture. Immediately dip coated ends of some cookies into **chocolate shot.** Set coated cookies on cooling rack over a piece of waxed paper.

Almond Spritz Cookies

4¾ cups sifted all-purpose flour
½ teaspoon baking powder
1 cup (about ⅓ lb.) blanched almonds
2 cups butter
½ teaspoon almond extract
1 cup sugar
1 egg, well beaten

1. Set out cookie sheets.
2. Sift together flour and baking powder and set aside.
3. Grate almonds and set aside.
4. Cream together butter and almond extract until butter is softened.
5. Add sugar gradually, creaming until fluffy after each addition.
6. Add egg gradually, beating well after each addition.
7. Blend in the grated nuts. Mixing well after each addition, blend in dry ingredients in fourths.
8. Fill a cookie press about two-thirds full with dough. Following manufacturer's directions, form cookies of varied shapes directly onto cookie sheets.
9. Bake at 350°F 12 to 15 min., or until cookies are golden yellow.
10. With spatula, carefully remove cookies to cooling racks; cool completely.

About 10 doz. cookies

Dreams

36	(about 1½oz.) whole blanched almonds
2	cups sifted all-purpose flour
1	teaspoon baking powder
1	cup butter
2	teaspoons vanilla extract
¾	cup sugar

1. Set out cookie sheets.
2. Set out almonds.
3. Sift together flour and baking powder and set aside.
4. Cream together butter and vanilla extract until butter is softened.
5. Add sugar gradually, creaming until fluffy after each addition.
6. Mixing well after each addition, blend in dry ingredients in fourths. Shape dough into small balls about 1 in. in diameter. Place on the cookie sheets. Press one whole almond onto the center of each cookie.
7. Bake at 325°F 20 to 25 min., or until cookies are golden brown.
8. Remove to cooling racks to cool completely.

About 3 doz. cookies

Berlin Wreaths

3	eggs
1	cup butter
½	teaspoon vanilla extract
½	cup sugar
2	egg yolks
2	cups sifted all-purpose flour
	Egg white, slightly beaten
	Sugar

1. Set out cookie sheets.
2. Hard-cook eggs.
3. While eggs are cooking, cream together butter and vanilla extract until butter is softened.
4. Add ½ cup sugar gradually, creaming until fluffy after each addition.
5. Cut the hard-cooked eggs into halves; remove egg yolks to a bowl. Mash them with a fork. Add egg yolk one at a time, blending in thoroughly.
6. Add the egg mixture in thirds to the creamed mixture, beating thoroughly after each addition.
7. Measure flour.
8. Add the sifted flour in fourths, beating thoroughly after each addition. Chill dough in refrigerator.
9. Cut off a small amount of dough and roll with hands into a strip about 4 in. long and ¼ in. thick. The ends of the strip should be slightly pointed. Overlap ends about ¼ in., forming a wreath. Brush with egg white.
10. Sprinkle lightly with sugar.
11. Place cookies on cookie sheets.
12. Bake at 350°F 10 to 12 min., or until cookies are golden yellow.
13. With spatula, carefully remove cookies to cooling racks; cool completely.

About 5 doz. cookies

Swedish Gingersnaps

Whole blanched almonds
(about 10)
1½ cups sifted all-purpose
flour
1 teaspoon baking soda
1½ teaspoons ginger
1 teaspoon cinnamon
¼ teaspoon cloves
½ cup butter
¾ cup sugar
1 egg, well beaten
1½ teaspoons dark corn syrup

1. Set out cookie sheets.
2. Set out almonds.
3. Sift together flour, baking soda, ginger, cinnamon and cloves and set aside.
4. Cream butter until softened.
5. Add sugar gradually, creaming until fluffy after each addition.
6. Add egg and dark corn syrup gradually, beating thoroughly after each addition.
7. Blend in dry ingredients in fourths, mixing thoroughly after addition. Chill in refrigerator several hours.
8. Remove some of the chilled dough and place on a lightly floured surface. Roll about 1/16 in. thick. Cut with lightly floured cookie cutters into various shapes. Cut almonds into small pieces and place one piece in the center of each cookie. Transfer cookies to cookie sheets. Repeat with remaining chilled dough.
9. Bake at 375°F 6 to 8 min.
10. Carefully remove cookies to cooling racks to cool completely.

About 7 doz. cookies

Medallion Cookies

Cream Filling (page 65)
4½ cups sifted all-purpose
flour
2 cups butter
¾ cup plus 2 tablespoons
sifted confectioners' sugar
1 egg
1 cup sifted confectioners'
sugar
½ teaspoon vanilla extract
Milk or cream (about 1
tablespoon or enough to
make a frosting that will
hold its shape)

1. Set out cookie sheets.
2. Prepare cream filling and chill.
3. Measure flour and set aside.
4. Cream butter until softened.
5. Add ¾ cup plus 2 tablespoons sifted confectioners' sugar gradually, creaming just until blended.
6. Blend egg in thoroughly.
7. Add the flour in fourths, blending thoroughly after each addition. Set aside for 20 min. (not in refrigerator).
8. Place one-third of the dough on a lightly floured surface. Roll about ¼ in. thick. Cut out cookies with a lightly floured 2-in. round cookie cutter. Place cookies on cookie sheets. Repeat for remaining dough.
9. Bake at 375°F about 10 min., or until cookies are lightly browned at edges.
10. With spatula, carefully remove cookies to cooling racks. Cool completely.
11. Meanwhile, combine 1 cup sifted confectioners' sugar and vanilla extract.
12. Add milk or cream.
13. When cookies are cooled completely, spoon about ¾ teaspoon of the filling onto one half the cookies. Top with the remaining cookies. Spread filled cookies with the confectioners' sugar mixture.
14. Cookies should be filled shortly before ready to serve. Fill only as many as will be needed. Refrigerate filled cookies if they are to be kept for any length of time before serving.

About 5 doz. cookies

Brown Sugar Cookies

2 **cups sifted all-purpose flour**
1 **cup butter**
¾ **cup firmly packed brown sugar**
1 **egg yolk**
Pecan or walnut halves

1. Set out cookies sheets.
2. Measure flour and set aside.
3. Cream butter until softened.
4. Add brown sugar gradually, creaming until fluffy after each addition.
5. Blend egg yolk in thoroughly.
6. Add the flour in fourths, mixing thoroughly after each addition. Shape dough into balls about ½ to ¾ in. thick. Place about 2 in. apart on the cookie sheets. Using the back of a fork, flatten cookies with crisscross marks.
7. Set out pecan or walnut halves.
8. Press a nut half onto the top of each cookie.
9. Bake at 375°F 8 to 10 min.
10. Cool cookies about 2 min. on cookie sheets. With spatula, remove cookies to cooling racks to cool completely.

About 7 doz. cookies

Danish Saddle Cookies

½ **cup finely chopped blanched almonds**
¼ **cup sugar**
2¼ **cups sifted all-purpose flour**
1 **cup butter**
1 **cup plus 2 tablespoons sugar**
2 **egg yolks, beaten**
1 **tablespoon water**

1. Set out cookie sheets. Wash and scrub a wooden stick about 1 in. in diameter and 12 to 18 in. long. Dry it thoroughly.
2. Mix together almonds and ¼ cup sugar and set aside.
3. Measure flour and set aside.
4. Cream 1 cup butter until softened.
5. Add 1 cup plus 2 tablespoons sugar gradually, creaming until fluffy after each addition.
6. Add the flour in fourths, mixing well after each addition.
7. Mix egg yolks and water together and set aside.
8. Place a small amount of dough at one time on a lightly floured surface and roll about ¼ in. thick. Cut into rectangles 3x1½ in. Place only 6 cookies at one time on the cookie sheet. Brush tops of cookies with the egg-yolk mixture and sprinkle cookies with the almond-sugar mixture.
9. Bake at 375°F 8 to 10 min., or until delicately browned.
10. Cool cookies slightly. Using a spatula, quickly remove cookies from cookie sheet and bend lengthwise over the stick. Cool (all six at one time) on stick; carefully remove cookies from the wooden stick. Repeat procedure until all of remaining dough is baked.

About 7 doz. cookies

Danish Cookies

2	cups sifted all-purpose flour
¼	teaspoon hartshorn (ammonium carbonate which is obtainable at any drugstore)
¾	cup butter
1	cup sugar
1	egg yolk
1	egg white
⅛	teaspoon salt
1¼	cups sifted confectioners' sugar

1. Set out cookie sheets.
2. Sift together flour and hartshorn and set aside.
3. Cream butter until softened.
4. Add sugar gradually, creaming until fluffy after each addition.
5. Blend egg yolk in thoroughly.
6. Add the dry ingredients in fourths, mixing thoroughly after each addition. Set aside.
7. Meanwhile, prepare a meringue by beating egg white and salt until frothy.
8. Add confectioners' sugar gradually, beating well after each addition.
9. Continue beating until very stiff peaks are formed. Cut dough into halves and set one-half aside. Roll one-half of the dough 1/8 in. thick on a lightly floured surface. Using a sharp knife, cut strips 1 in. wide. Cut each strip into diamond-shaped pieces by making diagonal cuts 1 in. apart. Place cookies on the cookie sheets and lightly spread cookies with the meringue. Repeat with the second half of the dough.
10. Bake at 375°F 10 min., or until lightly browned.
11. Cool cookies on cookie sheets about 2 min. Using a spatula, carefully remove cookies to cooling racks to cool completely.

About 6 doz. cookies

Sand Tarts

2	cups sifted all-purpose flour
⅓	cup (about 2 oz.) blanched almonds
1	cup butter
¼	teaspoon almond extract
¾	cup sugar
1	egg, beaten

1. Set out sandbakkelse molds and cookie sheets.
2. Measure flour and set aside.
3. Chop almonds very finely and set aside.
4. Cream butter and almond extract together until butter is softened.
5. Add sugar gradually, creaming just until blended.
6. Blend in egg.
7. Add the flour in fourths, blending well after each addition. Blend in the chopped almonds. Chill dough in refrigerator.
8. Remove a portion of the dough from refrigerator and return remaining dough to continue chilling. Place about 2 teaspoons dough into each mold. Using the thumb, firmly press dough into each mold, coating the bottom and sides evenly. Place molds on the cookie sheets. Repeat with the remaining dough.
9. Bake at 375°F 6 to 8 min. or until sand tarts are golden brown.
10. Immediately invert molds onto a smooth surface. Cool slightly. To remove sand tart from mold. hold the mold in the hand and tap lightly but sharply with the back of a spoon. Remove pan and place sand tarts on a smooth surface to cool completely.
11. Serve sand tarts inverted. Or turn sand tarts right side up and fill with jam, jelly, or whipped cream.

About 5 doz. cookies

Norwegian Cones

1½	cups sifted all-purpose flour
½	cup cornstarch
1½	teaspoons cardamom
1	cup butter
1¼	cups sugar
3	egg yolks
3	egg whites
⅛	teaspoon salt

1. Set out a krumkaker iron (usually available in the housewares section of a department store).
2. Sift together flour, cornstarch and cardamom into a bowl.
3. Cream butter until softened.
4. Add sugar gradually, creaming until fluffy after each addition.
5. Beat in egg yolks, one at a time, until thoroughly blended.
6. Add the dry ingredients in fourths, mixing well after each addition.
7. Beat egg whites and salt until stiff, not dry, peaks are formed.
8. Spread the beaten egg whites over batter and gently fold together.
9. Heat krumkaker iron until a drop of water "sputters" on its hot surface. Spoon about 1½ to 2 teaspoons batter onto hot iron. Close the krumkaker iron and cook on each side for a few seconds or until lightly browned. Immediately remove wafer with a spatula and roll into a cone. Cool completely.
10 Serve cones plain.

About 4 doz. cones

Filled Norwegian Cones: Follow recipe for Norwegian Cones. Fill cones with sweetened fresh **berries** or **Sweetened Whipped Cream.** If desired, garnish whipped cream with strips of **candied orange peel.**

Moon Cakes

1¼	cup flour
7	oz. butter
1	tsp. acetone

For brushing:
Egg white

Decoration:
Granulated sugar

1. Work together flour and butter on a pastry-board. Add acetone. Work the dough together and put it in a cold place to set.
2. Roll out the dough and cut out half moons with cookie cutters.
3. Brush the cakes with egg white, dip them in granulated sugar. Let the cakes stand about 15 minutes before baking them.
4. Bake the cakes in a 400°F oven for 6-8 minutes.

Yield: 100

Cinnamon Hearts

7	oz. butter
3	oz. sugar
2	cups flour
1	egg yolk

Decoration:
Egg white
Cinnamon
Sugar

1. Mix flour and sugar and cut in butter on a pastry-board. Add the egg yolks and work the dough together quickly. Put in cold place for a while.
2. Roll out the dough and cut out cookie cutter hearts. Brush them with lightly whipped egg white. Dip the cakes in a mixture of sugar and cinnamon. Bake in a 325°F oven for 10-12 minutes.

Yield: 75

Granny's Soft Gingerbread

½	cup butter
2	eggs
1	cup dark brown sugar
2	tsp. cinnamon
1	tsp. cardamom
1	tsp. ginger
½	tsp. ground cloves
1	tsp. baking powder
1½	cups flour
3	oz. heavy cream
3	oz. red raspberry jam
	bread crumbs

1. Melt the butter and let it cool.
2. Beat eggs and sugar until fluffy.
3. Combine flour, spices and baking powder and stir into the batter together with cream and jam.
4. Finally add the melted butter.
5. Pour the batter into a well greased 1½ qt. cake pan sprinkled with fine bread crumbs. Bake the cake in a 325°F. oven for about 1 hour. Test with a skewer. Allow to cool 10 minutes then remove from pan and place on cake rack.

Danish Hearts

Puff Pastry:

1	cup flour
2	oz. sugar
1	egg yolk
3½	oz. butter

Filling:

6	oz. cream
2	egg yolks
½	tbsp. sugar
½	tbsp. corn flour

Decoration:

confectioner's sugar
cherries
raspberries or strawberries

1. Blend flour, butter, egg yolk and sugar on a pastry board and work quickly into a dough.
2. Roll out the dough and line ⅔ of a greased heart-shaped pan with the paste.
3. Mix the ingredients for the filling and simmer on low heat until thickened. Let the cream cool.
4. Distribute the cream in the pans. Roll out the rest of the dough and put on top. Pinch the edges.
5. Bake the cakes in a 350°F for about 18 minutes. Remove the cakes and let them get cold.
6. Sift on the confectioner's sugar and decorate with berries.

Yield: 12

Jam Cakes

8	oz. butter
4	oz. sugar
1¼	cups flour

Filling:

Raspberry Jam or Jelly

1. Work together the butter, sugar and flour quickly. Shape into a roll about 2″ in diameter and put it in a cold place for a while.
2. Cut the roll in about 1″ thick slices with a sharp knife. Make a hole in the middle and fill it with jam or jelly.
3. Bake the cakes in a 350°F oven for about 10 minutes.

Beverages

Coffee is the leading beverage of Scandinavia and the Scandinavians the leading coffee-drinkers of the world. Social drinking of alcoholic beverages is ceremonious, and a toast—a cordial "Skål!"—accompanies every sip of aquavit or punch.

Vanilla Confectioners' Sugar

Confectioners' sugar
1 vanilla bean, about 9 in. long

1. Set out a 1 to 2-qt. container having a tight-fitting cover. Fill with confectioners' sugar.
2. Wipe vanilla bean with a clean, damp cloth and dry.
3. Cut vanilla bean into quarters lengthwise; cut quarters crosswise into thirds. Poke pieces of vanilla bean down into the sugar at irregular intervals. Cover container tightly and store.

Note: The longer sugar stands, the richer will be the vanilla flavor. If tightly covered, sugar may be stored for several months. When necessary, add more sugar to jar. Replace vanilla bean when aroma is gone.

Coffee

Drip Coffee—Preheat coffee maker with boiling water. Drain. For each standard measuring cup of **water** (use freshly drawn cold water and boil), using standard measuring spoons, measure 2 tablespoons **drip grind coffee.** Spoon into filter section of drip coffee maker.

Pour into upper container measured, freshly **boiling water.** Cover. Allow water to drip through coffee grounds, keeping coffee maker over low heat 5 to 8 min., or while coffee is dripping. Do not let coffe boil at any time. Remove coffee compartment; stir and cover the brew. If coffee cannot be served immediately, place coffee maker over low heat.

Percolated Coffee—Use **regular grind coffee.** Follow recipe for Drip Coffee for amount of coffee and water to use. Spoon into strainer basket of coffee maker. Measure fresh cold water into bottom of percolator. Insert basket into coffee maker. Cover.

Place over heat and when percolating begins, reduce heat to low so percolating will be gentle and slow. Timing varies from 5 to 10 min. after percolation starts. It is wise to experiment to determine exact timing for the amount of coffee generally made in your percolator. Larger amounts of coffee require the longer timing.

Remove coffee basket, cover coffee maker and keep coffee hot over low heat. Do not let boil.

Steeped Coffee— Use **regular grind coffee.** Follow recipe for Drip Coffee for amount of coffee and water to use. Put into coffee maker. To clarify this coffee, mix in 1 teaspoon slightly **beaten egg** for each 2 tablespoons coffee used. Measure and add fresh cold water.

Bring very slowly to boiling, stirring occasionally. Remove from heat at once. Pour ¼ cup **water** down spout to settle grounds. Let stand 3 to 5 min. without heat. Strain coffee through a fine strainer into a server which has been preheated with boiling water. If necessary to keet hot, let coffee stand over low heat without boiling.

Vacuum Drip Coffee— Use **drip** or **vacuum grind coffee.** Follow recipe for Drip Coffee for amount of coffee and water to use.

Specific directions for making vary according to the type of coffee maker used. Usually, freshly drawn cold water is measured and poured into the decanter or lower bowl of the coffee maker. Coffee is measured into upper bowl. Cover.

Place coffee maker over moderate to low heat. When all but a small amount of water has risen to upper bowl, remove coffee maker from heat. Remove top bowl when the brew has run into decanter. Cover. Serve immediately or keep hot over very low heat. Do not boil at any time.

Glögg

1	cup (about 5 oz.) almonds
1	bottle (25 oz.) Aquavit
1	bottle (25 oz.) claret
6	2½-in. cinnamon sticks
1	cup (about 4 oz.) dark seedless raisins
6	pieces candied orange or lemon peel
12	whole cloves
12	cardamom seeds, peeled
1	cup loaf sugar

1. Blanch almonds.
2. Empty aquavit and claret into a large saucepan or sauce pot.
3. Add the almonds, cinnamon sticks, raisins, orange or lemon peel, whole cloves and cardamom seeds.
4. Bring slowly to boiling. Reduce heat and simmer 10 min. Remove saucepan from heat. Put loaf sugar into a large sieve.
5. Place sieve over saucepan. Using a ladle or large spoon, pour some of the mixture from the saucepan over the sugar. Ignite the sugar with a match. Continue to pour the liquid over the sugar until the sugar has completely melted. The liquid will be flaming. If necessary, extinguish flame by placing cover over saucepan.
6. Serve Glögg hot in mugs or punch glasses. Be sure there are some raisins and almonds in each portion.

10 to 15 servings

Note: Glögg may be prepared days in advance and stored in bottles. When ready to serve, heat thoroughly (do not boil). Or if there is some Glögg left it may be stored for future use.

Lemonade

½	cup lemon juice
½-¾	cup sugar
3-4	cups water

1. Mix lemon juice and sugar. Stir until sugar melts. Add water.
2. Serve ice cold with crushed ice or ice cubes.

Makes 1 quart.

Mixed Fruit Punch

1	can pineapple juice
1	can grapefruit juice
1	can frozen concentrated orange juice
4-6	cups water
	juice of 1 lemon
1	bottle club soda
1-2	lemons or oranges, sliced
1	package frozen strawberries or grapes

1. Mix all ingredients.

Index

SCANDINAVIAN INDEX

ENGLISH INDEX